Gourds in Motion

Simple Techniques to Make Gourd Projects Move

C. Angela Mohr

SCHIFFER PUBLISHING
4880 Lower Valley Road • Atglen, PA 19310

To Mary Mohr, a woman of lifelong strength, courage, and persistence who has always been a mover and a shaker not stopped by momentary setbacks. Not one to stand still, Mary is a woman of action whom I am humbled and proud to call Mom.

Other Schiffer Books by the Author:

Making Gourd Ornaments, 978-0-7643-2716-2, $12.95

Creating Snowflake Art: Designing Original Papercuttings, 978-0-7643-2971-5, $12.99

Apples to Apples: Basic Techniques for Decorating Gourds, 978-0-7643-3621-8, $19.99

Making More Gourd Ornaments, 978-0-7643-3620-1, $19.99

Gourd Art Basics: The Complete Guide to Cleaning, Preparation, and Repair, 978-0-7643-2829-9, $14.99

Gourd Puppets and Dolls: A Do-It-Yourself for Crafters, 978-0-7643-2868-8, $15.00

Historic Gourd Craft: How to Make Traditional Vessels, 978-0-7643-2830-5, $15.00

Making Gourd Headpieces: Decorating and Creating Headgear for Every Occasion, 978-0-7643-2869-5, $15.00

Library of Congress Control Number: 2019936344

Photography by Bob Smith
Designed by Ashley Millhouse
Cover design by Brenda McCallum
Type set in Univers/Helvetica Neue

ISBN: 978-0-7643-5832-6
Printed in China

Published by Schiffer Publishing, Ltd.
4880 Lower Valley Road
Atglen, PA 19310
Phone: (610) 593-1777; Fax: (610) 593-2002
E-mail: Info@schifferbooks.com
Web: www.schifferbooks.com

CONTENTS

FOREWORD

For centuries, toys have been used to amuse and educate youngsters in preparation for adulthood. Additionally, mechanical devices have been innovated as entertainments for wealthy adults with the resources to hire inventors. Although locally available materials around the house and farm have been used to make toys, how could gourds have been used to make them? There is a body of knowledge regarding toy and mechanical fascinations throughout time, but the connection between play toys and gourds has not been explored as a crafting option. In this book, gourds are used to mimic the shape, size, and purpose of the original toy. Knowing how gourds can be used to make moving toys and desktop kinetic sculptures offers possibilities for adding movement to a gourd project, thereby providing inspiration for modern gourd crafters to explore new avenues for their creative talents.

SUPPLIES FOR PROJECTS

As with my other gourd how-to books, the projects here are intended as stepping stones to your own creative pursuits. The tools are simple devices you probably already have or can make expediently. Others can be purchased at a local hardware or big-box store. I buy almost all my stuff from the Dollar Tree stores, my local hardware store, and American Science Surplus. Don't misunderstand me—there are AMAZING tools that gourd enthusiasts use, with which they achieve AMAZING results, far better than what I can produce. However, I prefer the innovation end of gourd art and craft, and that requires experimentation, trial and error, and a fair number of mistakes. In my personal projects, I don't mind if I break a $5 tool to achieve a goal, but if I spent a hundred dollars on a tool, there would be more heartache in the garage. I would encourage you to start simple. This is what I have on my workbenches to use on a daily basis (listed alphabetically):

- ❑ Adhesives: White glue, wood glue, E6000, Super Glue Gel. Note—Unlike Super Glue, Super Glue Gel is made for porous surfaces, which gourds and wooden dowels are. The point of contact is instant and strong. However, if the fear of getting it on your fingers is not for you, then use wood glue. Wood glue takes longer to dry, of course, but it leaves time for readjustment.
- ❑ Color: Craft paints, alcohol ink, spray paints
- ❑ Color applicators: Brushes, sponges, cotton swabs
- ❑ Dremel with various bits
- ❑ Full-size drill with various bits AND a set of hole-cutting bits
- ❑ Gourds: Miniature bottleneck, banana, spinner, egg, long-handled dipper, swan, and kettle. Gourd scraps from other projects, especially entry holes from birdhouse projects.
- ❑ Hairnets (specific to the fish project)
- ❑ Mini craft saw
- ❑ Pieces of leather
- ❑ Plastic hummingbird feeders and sand or small-particle gravel (specific to the hourglass project)
- ❑ Pliers (needlenose and flathead) to cut and curl wire
- ❑ Sandpapers, files
- ❑ Sharpies
- ❑ Wires: florist wire, wire coat hanger (specific to the skyhook), eye screws
- ❑ Woodburning tool—chisel tip and a round top
- ❑ Wooden dowels: ¾", ¼", skewers
- ❑ X-ACTO knives with #11 blades—I store them embedded into a wine cork to protect the tips (and me)
- ❑ Yarn, string, rope

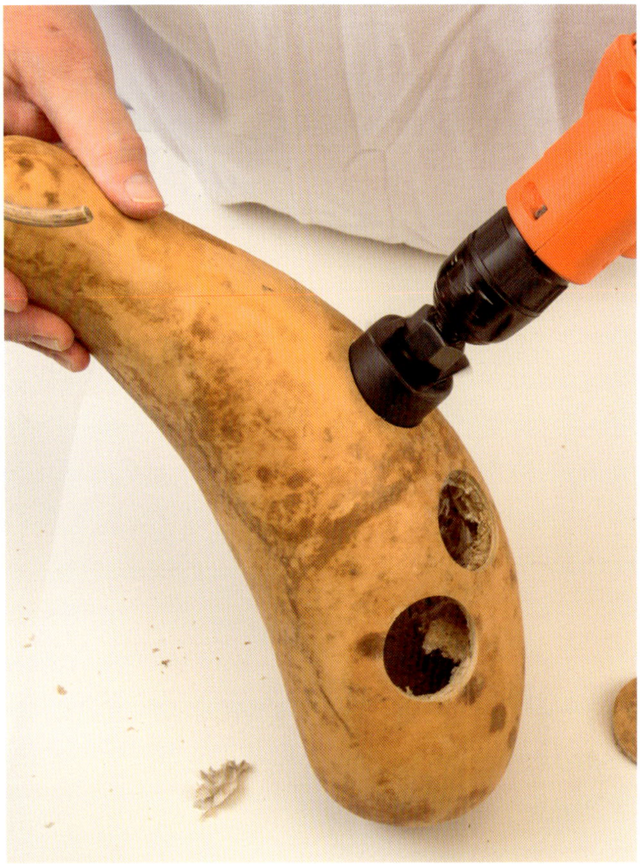

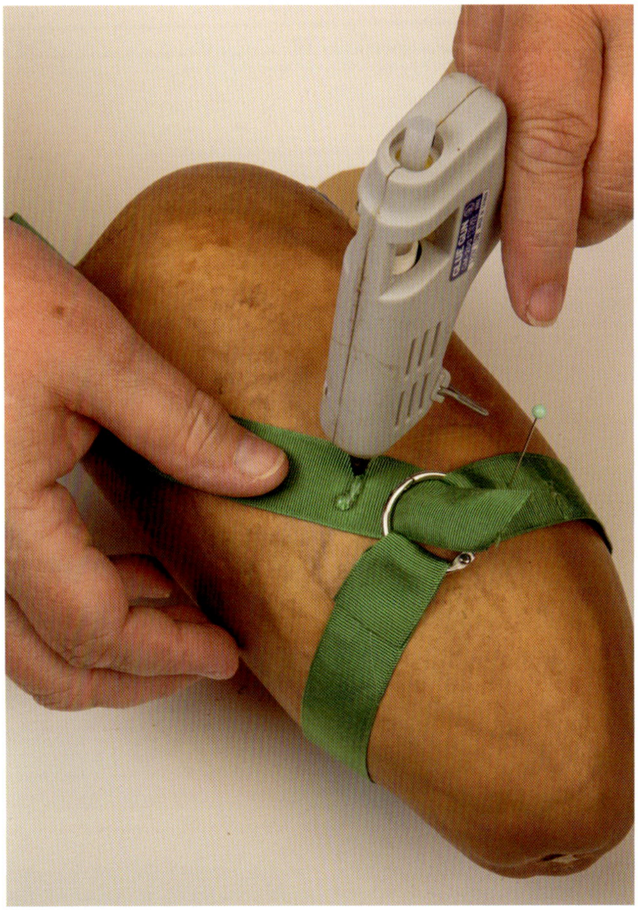

INTRODUCTION

Many pieces of gourd art and craft are elaborately decorated items of visual beauty. An equal number are utilitarian in nature for basic household or garden needs, such as simply produced scoops, birdhouses, or water sprinklers. Either way, gourd art and craft items are usually stationary.

Dan Wolpert of the University of Cambridge says, "We have a brain for one reason and one reason only—and that's to produce adaptable and complex movements." (Medder, accessed 2018).

Although this quote is part of research explaining why humans need physical movement for day-to-day living, it may explain why moving objects are as interesting for children playing with toys for instruction purposes (McMahon 2014) as they are for adults enjoying small desktop toys during moments of thought and destressing in an otherwise long and trying day of work (Lasky 2015). Although there are many examples of complicated and meticulously machined pieces of kinetic art available, enjoying "the simple quirkiness and wit of a mechanical toy" (Peppé 2015) can be applied to a gourd toy. Nothing is quirkier than gourds! Whether educational in nature or items of idle distraction, moving toys have a long history dating back to ancient Greece, when the inventor Daedalus mechanized statues to imitate human actions. Such a

Gourd art can be both decorative and practical but is distinguished by the artist's style, techniques, and use of media.

Utilitarian gourds are functional pieces of gourds made to serve a day-to-day purpose.

statue was obviously commissioned by a wealthy patron and not for children. Eventually, the industrial age and mass production techniques made the production of kinetic pieces of art easier and less expensive to produce. Thus, moving toys went from expensive adult entertainments to children toys (Addams n.d.).

Even during the industrial age, as for generations before, objects made for children's play were often made using locally accessible materials or items around the house or farm, such as bits of cloth, string, sticks of wood, or corn cobs (Bledsoe 2002). Using this logic, I propose that gourds could have been used to make toys, either reproductions of traditional playthings or more-elaborate mechanical devices using technology concepts. In fact, by using simple tools purchased inexpensively, locally accessed gourds, and a little imagination sprinkled with patience, gourds seem a natural consideration for making a plaything. Certainly a plaything that moves would be an added bonus!

Visit www.schifferbooks.com/gourdsinmotion to see a gallery of gourds in motion!

BEGIN AT THE BEGINNING

Gourds are the inedible part of the squash family. In fact, there are three types, according the American Gourd Society (2018): cucurbita—colorful, small gourds seen in stores and at farm markets in the fall; lagenaria—hard-shelled gourds that grow green on the vine but dehydrate to thick-shelled brown or tan shapes used for crafting purposes; and luffa—thin-shelled fruits of plants with fibrous interiors, used as sponges once dehydrated. For purposes of making objects that move, this book will focus mostly on lagenaria and cucurbita gourds, which tend to have a wood-like wall structure when dehydrated: kettle, banana, egg, spinner, and dipper gourds, with scraps from a variety of other gourds left in the shed from past projects.

Gourds are planted and grow in full sunshine all summer and into the fall, when the first couple of frosts shrivel the vine. The gourds are then harvested and put in a well-ventilated place off the ground to dehydrate for a season or two. In the process, they will get moldy and generally distasteful visually. However, as long as they hold their shape and become lighter in weight, they are dehydrating according to plan. The seeds inside may or may not be loose enough to hear rattling when the gourd is shaken, but thumping a knuckle against the wall will help determine if it is ready to prepare for an art or craft project. The wall will be hard and the gourd will sound hollow. The deeper the pitch when thumped, the thicker the wall. When all this happens, it is time to prepare it for making a project. In my area in Virginia, I can plant in late May, and by the following April or May it will be time to use the gourds for building projects.

A faster way to start on a gourd project is to buy the prepared gourds at a gourd festival or gourd farm. This plan works on a couple of levels: you get immediate access to gourds, and you get to choose what you want instead of being at the mercy of what grew in the yard (sometimes having cross-pollinated into unplanned shapes). Your choice will depend on schedule, needs, and level of patience. When I am on a roll, and I want specific gourds, I just make a trip to the nearest gourd farm. Otherwise, I have learned to buy up gourds when I find them and keep them in labeled bins in the garage. Compulsive? Maybe. A sign of gourd hoarding? Certainly. Am I happy when I can put my hand on what I want? Absolutely!

Dehydrated gourds

A gourd with a cleaned area

CLEANING

If you have not obtained previously prepared gourds, the start of the prep process is washing the debris off the surface of the gourd and cleaning the stem. This is done by dampening the gourd long enough to soften the surface dirt so it can be scrubbed off using a pot scrubby or sanding sponge. The gourds can float in a bucket of water, be left out in the rain, or be covered with a wet towel. Although contact with water for extended periods of time is not a good idea for dehydrated gourds, short time spans used for softening the surface dirt and mold will not harm the gourd as long as there are no cracks in the wall, where water can seep in and settle. It is the constant contact with moisture that makes an issue for any natural product, including gourds. The scrubbing time is at hand when a sample area reveals a clean patch of gourd surface when tested (*see* right hand image on p. 11).

Having said this, keep in mind that new techniques evolve all the time. Using a small handheld power washer is a convenient way to wash off softened dirt and molds. I have used an old wringer washer on a slow/soaker setting to gently agitate gourds, which bumps the gourds together, knocking off the dirt. Currently there is a process for cleaning gourds by using damp soil (The Gourd, 2018). Fill a storage bin with damp—not wet—potting soil or dirt and bury the gourds to be cleaned for a couple of days. Keep in mind this is not all-over contact with water, in the way that submerging in water would be. This process allows the dampness to soften the surface debris in a slower, more controlled way. Do test patches to see when the time is right for wiping the surface.

In any of these ways, there may be still be the occasional tiny piece of gourd skin tightly adhering to the surface. I run a slow stream of water over a cleaned gourd to show a smooth sheet of wet across the surface. Any leftover bits on the surface will be revealed as an interruption in the water. When I see a tiny spot of something, I use the back of a butter knife to pop it off the surface. As a cautionary note: The gourd surface will often become mottled in the drying process. Do not confuse surface mottling, which is the natural coloring of the gourd wall, with surface dirt.

At the end of the cleaning process, remember to use a small brush to clean the stem for a finished appearance. This step is often forgotten by beginners eager to start a project. Afterward, let the gourd dry completely before starting the decorating or cutting.

Once the gourd surface has been cleaned of dirt and mold, the surface may show various patterns of discoloring, called mottling. These were made by the dehydration process. Sometimes the variations can add to the design of a piece, or sometimes an artist will want a gourd without natural marking.

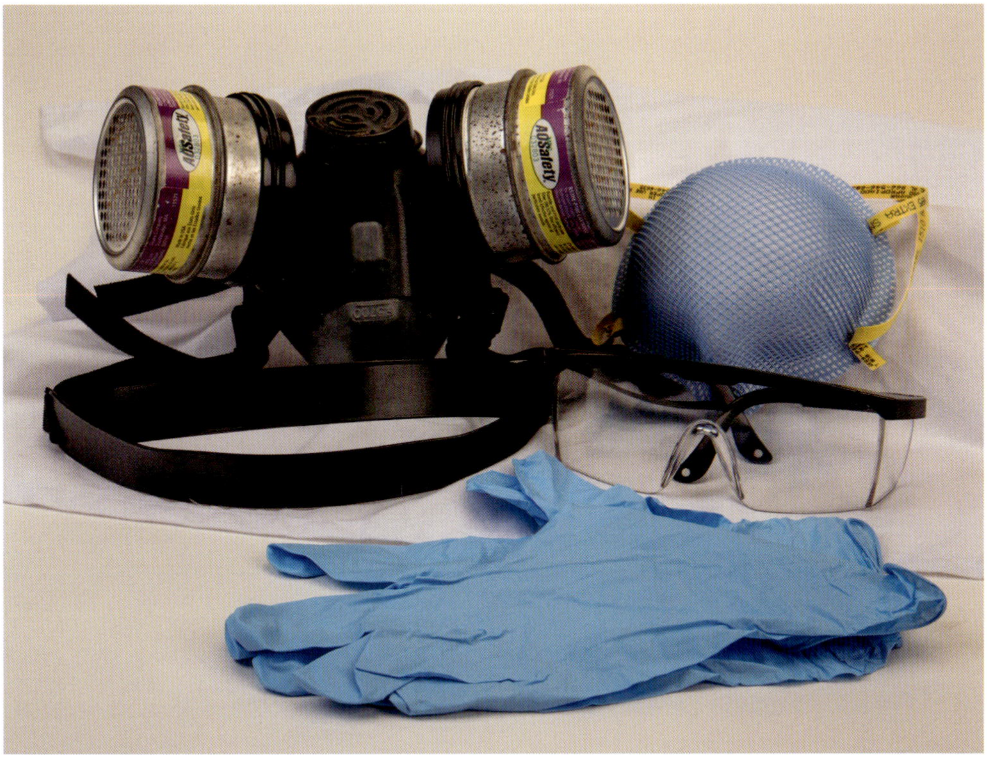

These are the protective supplies I keep at the workshop table or carry with me when I teach classes. Always err on the side of overprotection!

OPENING AND GUTTING

If the project involves opening the gourd, such as for a bowl or jar, make sure to use a facial mask at the very least and a respirator if possible. Opening the gourd releases gourd dust from the line of cutting, as well as small airborne spores from whatever has developed inside the gourd. In many cases the interior is an unknown until it is opened, and by then it would be too late if sinus, mouth, and eye protection had not been worn. Forewarned is forearmed!

To open the gourd, draw a cutting line to follow and then make a slit on the line, big enough for a saw blade to get through by using a knife or flathead screwdriver. Slip the saw blade into the slit and begin cutting the wall along the line. Separate the two pieces from each other slowly to see what's inside, preferably over a trash can with a lid, so the contents can be thrown away and covered immediately if they're all black and moldy. However, if the pith is white and fluffy and the seeds look plump, you may want to keep it. I plant pith with the seeds as an added moisture bonus during the hot and dry summer season, since it absorbs water and can release it slowly as the ground dries.

Gutting is the process of clearing the interior and, if needed, making the walls smooth enough for the project at hand. Using a scraper such as a grapefruit spoon or even a hammered-flat bottle cap can roughly take off anything clinging to the walls. Sandpapers, sanding sponges, files, and a variety of drill bits with wire or acrylic brushes can continue to take away surface area until the desired amount of smoothness is reached. THIS is the time when the breathing precautions are vital! Wear masks or respirators and eye goggles in a well-ventilated area. When finished, vacuum or use a tack cloth to whisk away any small dust particles left behind in the preparation process.

GOURD WORK AND WOODWORKING

Except for the washing part, preparation and production of gourds for art and craft are very similar to what is done when using wood for a project. Sawing, drilling, sanding, and attending to dust all are parts of the process that woodworkers use. The tools would be similar as well. In instances when miniature gourds are used, there would be a need for miniature versions of full-sized woodworking tools such as a mini craft saw or Dremel instead of a full-sized jigsaw or drill, but the same concepts apply. Glues, paints, and sealants all seem to translate from one to the other. What about dowels, knives, files, hole cutters, grommets, colored wires, science class materials, and even broken pieces of jewelry? When trying to complete a task, gourd enthusiasts consider what artisans in other craft fields use, and often adapt and apply those tools and techniques to gourd work. Woodworking and gourd work seem to correlate easily, but so will other mediums! In my opinion, begin with common tools accessed locally and see what can be done before investing in specialized tools until you are sure the investment is worth the result.

USING THE GOURDS

The best advice for making a moving-gourd project comes from Richard Race (2014): "A good deal of trial and error may be involved in getting a new design to work properly. See that as part of the fun." I couldn't agree more—focus on the process. Once your creation is done, there will be no substitution for the sheer delight of watching it move. Any time spent making adjustments to get there will be worth it! Let's start with some basic gourd figures to use when making moving-gourd projects. A crafter can get several project results from a limited number of gourd shapes, in this case banana, miniature bottleneck, spinner, and egg gourds. These examples are intended to show variation, so when going through your stash of gourds and supplies at home for one project or another, make adjustments as needed. What works for one project may not be suitable for another. For example, a banana gourd that makes a good shape for a race car may not be a good choice for an angel's body . . . or may be. Critical thinking is an individual phenomenon! These are the gourd ideas I use to make experiments—the same gourds are used in a variety of ways. Feel free to use these as starting points.

CARROT

Let's get started with banana gourds. For carrots, use a sponge to streak orange paint around a banana gourd. The streaking gives a color variation that flat color doesn't provide.

Drill a hole at the end for the foliage.

Insert green fiber of some kind for the vegetable foliage.

Here are some examples of green fiber: yarn, Easter basket stuffing, and raffia.

FISH

To start a fish, sponge a thin layer of paint onto the area intended as the fish's belly.

Stretch a hairnet over the top side of the banana gourd. Pull it tight and hold it in place with a clothespin.

Dot alcohol ink onto the net fibers, which will spread along the netting and color the fish. I am layering blue on top of purple. Let dry completely and remove the net.

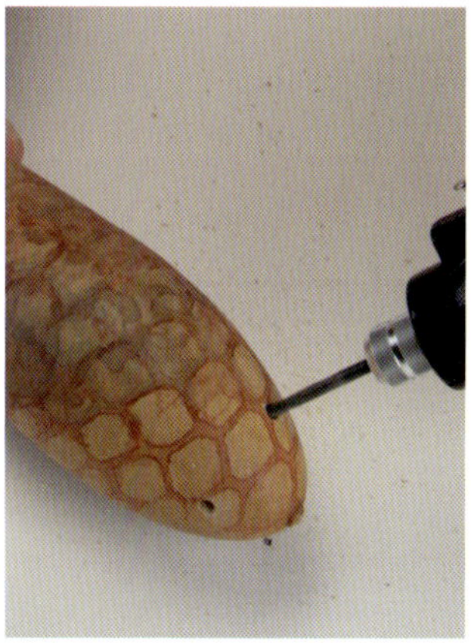

Drill holes for the eyes.

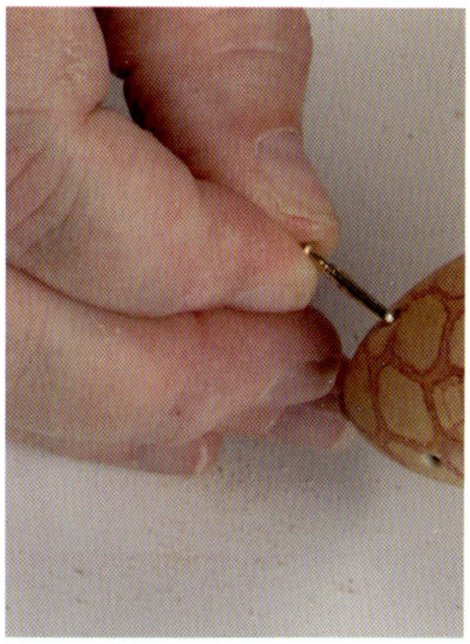

Dip brass nails into an epoxy such as E6000 before pushing them into the eyeholes.

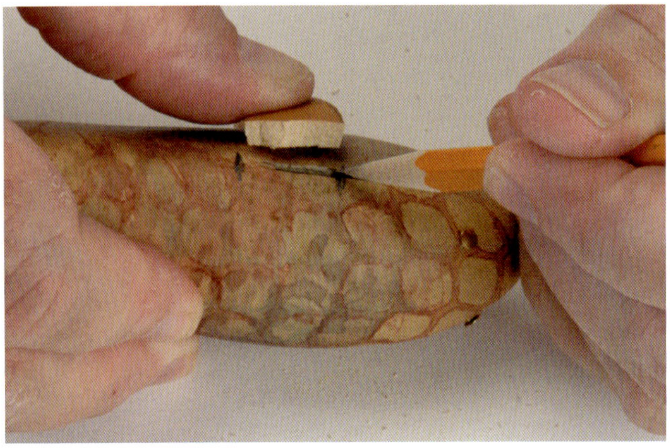

Measure and mark where triangle-shaped scraps can be inserted on the sides of the gourd for fins.

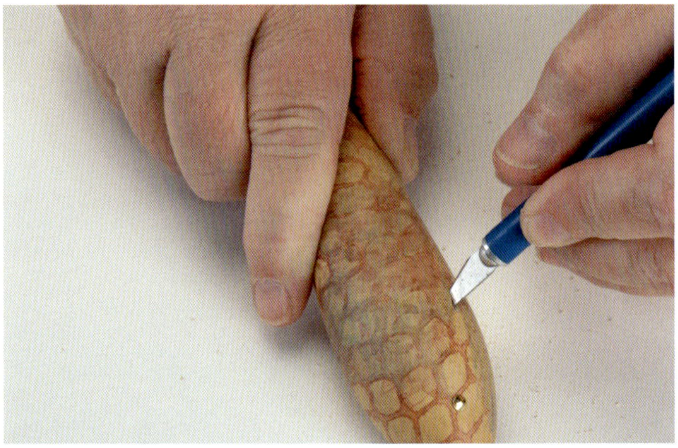

Cut slits into the sides of the gourd with an X-ACTO knife for the fins.

Use a small drill to grind out the line made with the knife.

Test, grind, test, and grind until there is a snug fit.

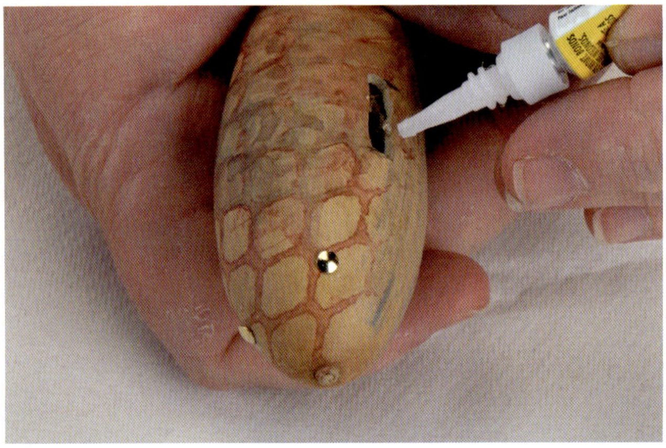

Super Glue Gel is made for porous surfaces.

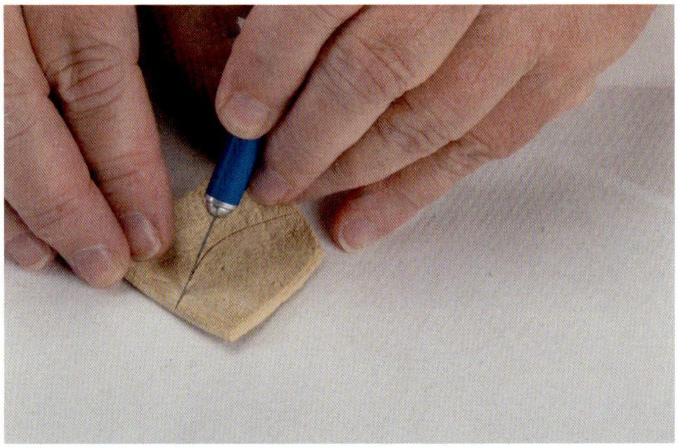

After fitting the side fins, make a tail fin by scoring the backside of a scrap with an X-ACTO knife. Scoring is running a cut line along a surface without cutting all the way through.

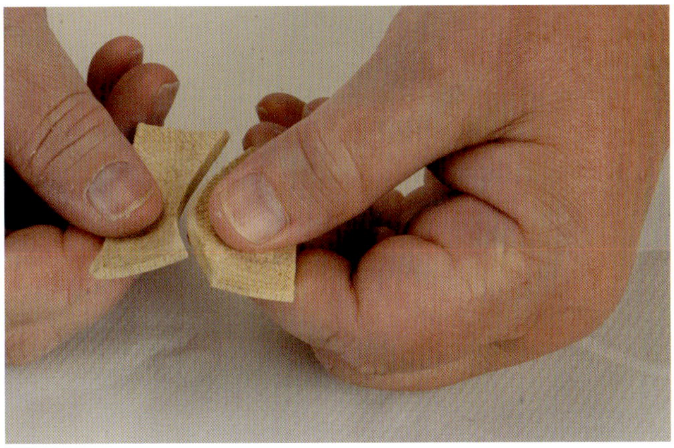

By scoring the backside, the scrap can be snapped apart.

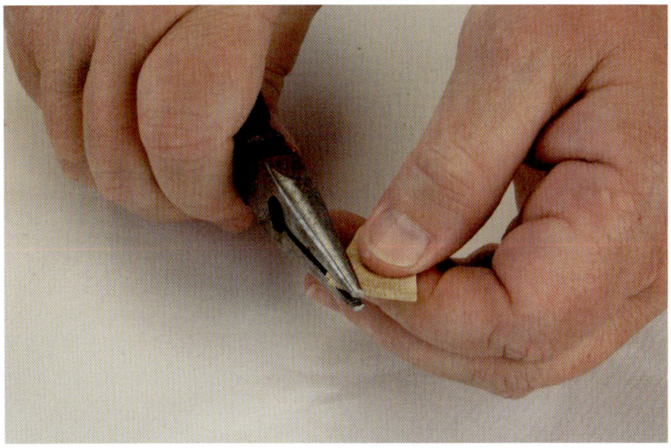

Shape the scrap broadly with needlenose pliers.

Sand it for final shaping.

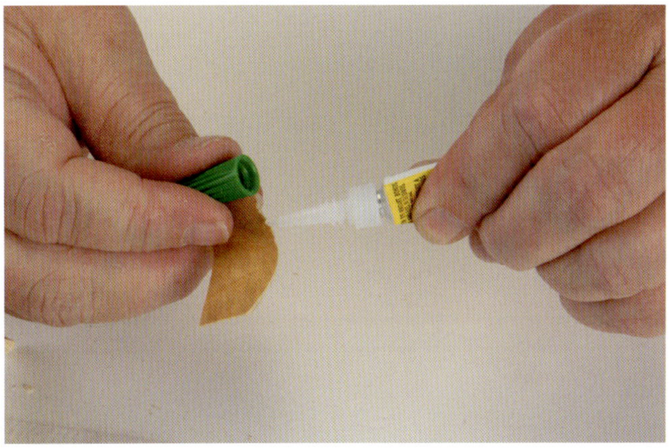

After sanding or cutting a groove into the stem end of the banana gourd, attach the tail fin.

Super Glue Gel makes fast work of this since there is usually little space for a deep-enough groove to support the tail fin for a long drying time.

Fish! You can probably imagine how further details can be added as you make your own.

ANGELS AND FAIRIES

Using miniature bottleneck gourds for angels and fairies is a matter of halos and wings. For an angel, begin with drilling a hole behind the stem area at the top of bottleneck gourd. This would be considered the back of the head of the angel.

Make a halo by wrapping a wire around a circular object, and twist the ends together. I'm using the cap of a paint bottle as my halo form.

Glue the twisted ends into the hole. Note: the twist of wire is important because the glue gets into the grooves of the twist and provides a tighter connection; straight wire tends to slip out.

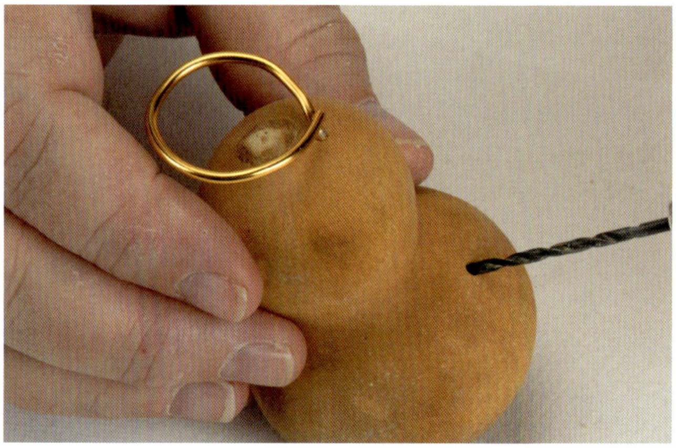

Drill another hole under the halo at around the shoulder area on the back.

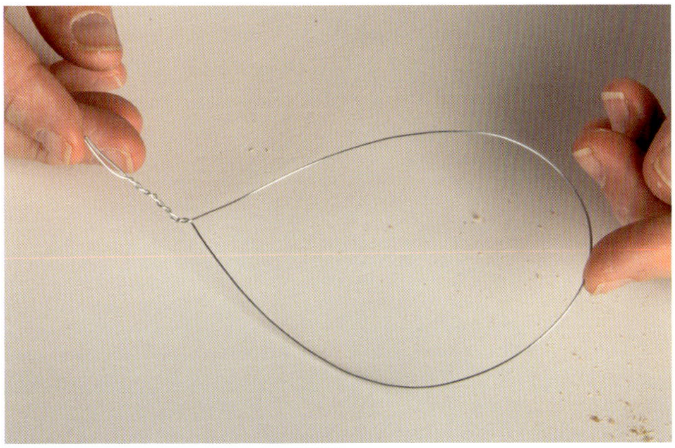

Make a loop of wire and twist the ends together.

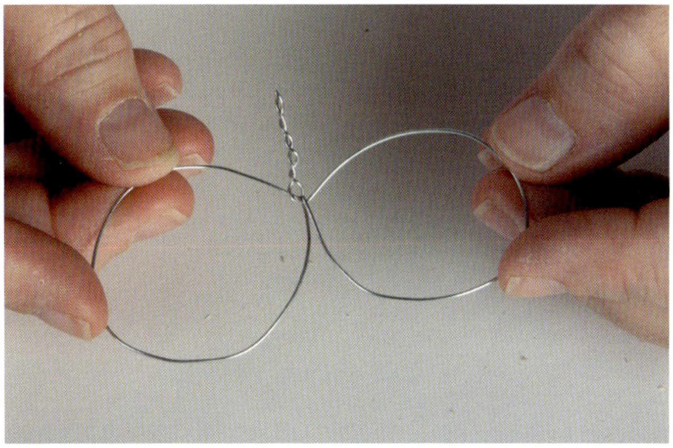

Collapse the loop and twist it into a figure 8.

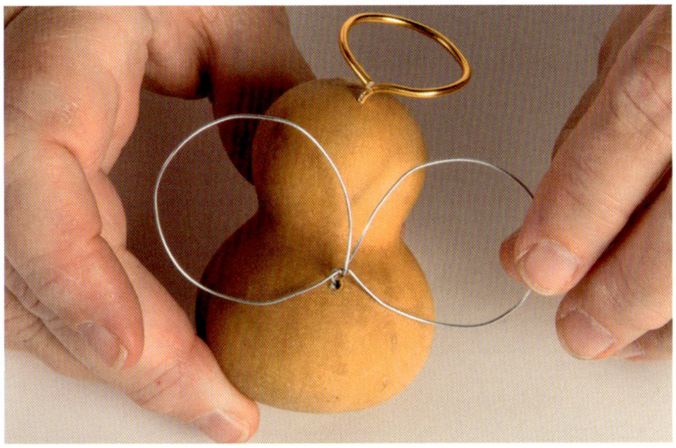

Insert the twisted ends of wire into the shoulder hole.

Fairy wings, on the other hand, are made with a wire turned into a double loop, one smaller than the other, before twisting the ends together.

Collapse both loops and twist to make a set of double wings.

This set of wings is inserted the same way as the angel wings.

SNOWMEN

Continuing with bottleneck gourds, let's move on to snowmen. Paint one white and dot black paint on it for the eyes, mouth, and buttons. I dip the end of a skewer or toothpick in the paint to make the dots.

Drill a hole for the nose.

Color the end of a toothpick orange. Cut off the tip and glue into the hole.

Drill holes in the side of the snowman for arms.

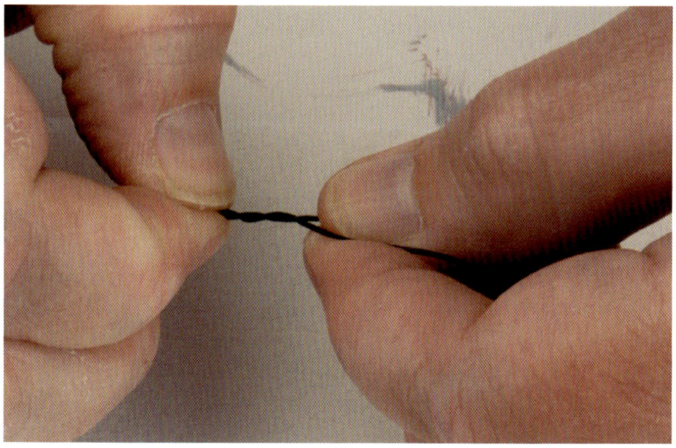

To make arms, fold a black-coated wire (the inexpensive kind, like what's at Dollar Tree) in half, and twist the end to make a branch finger.

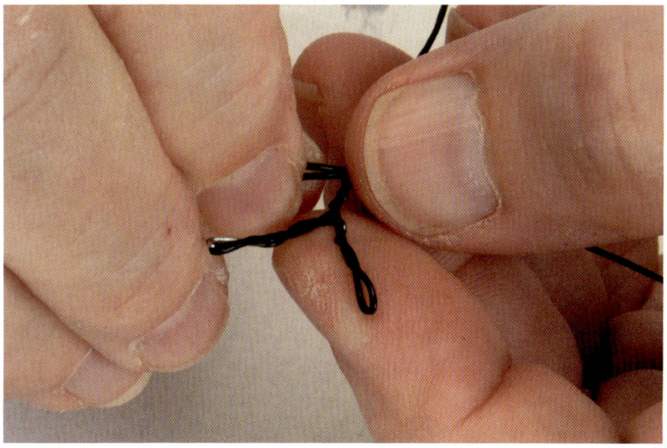

Twist a second loop of wire near it to make another branch finger. Note: There's no need to be symmetrical. Tree branches are irregular.

Twist the ends of the wire together for the branch arm, and glue into one of the holes made at the sides of the gourd.

POSEABLE PEOPLE

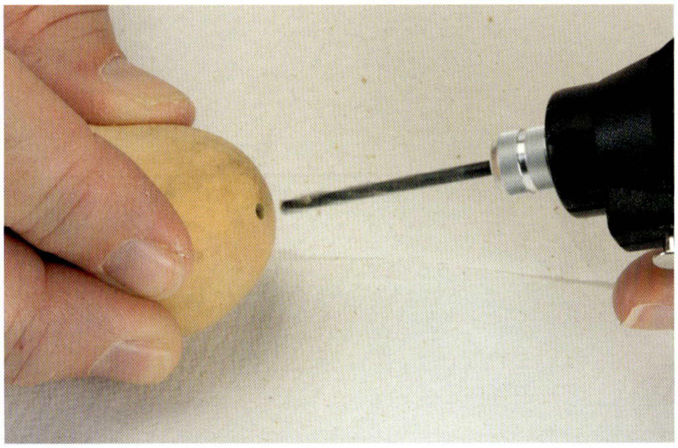

Spinner gourds are small and terrific for moving projects. To make poseable people, begin with a drilling a hole on each side of the spinner gourd, so the bottom is the back of the head and the stem end is the nose.

Put about a yard of wire through the holes of the gourd, so the stem end faces the front as the nose. Bring the wire at the top hole down the backside to meet the wire at the bottom hole. Adjust the wires so they are about the same length.

Twist the wires together at the neck.

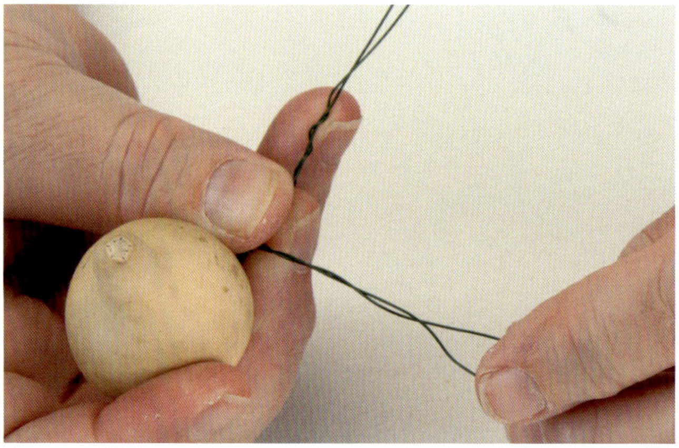

Twist the loops to make arms, but leaving a small loop at the ends for hands.

Use one wire to make two loops for arms, and twist together at the neck.

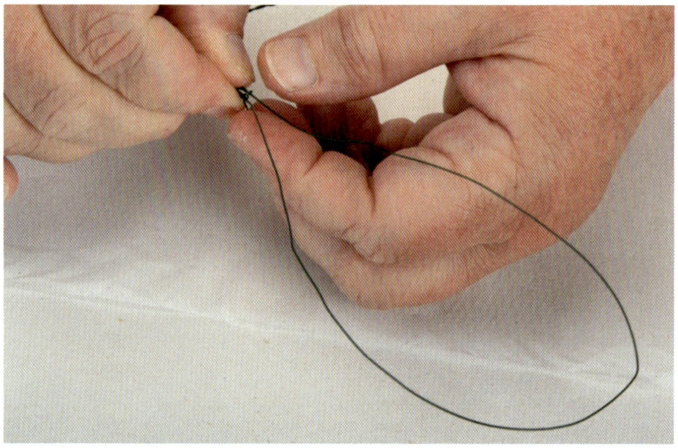

Use the long wire to a make a big loop that will be collapsed at the middle and twisted for the legs.

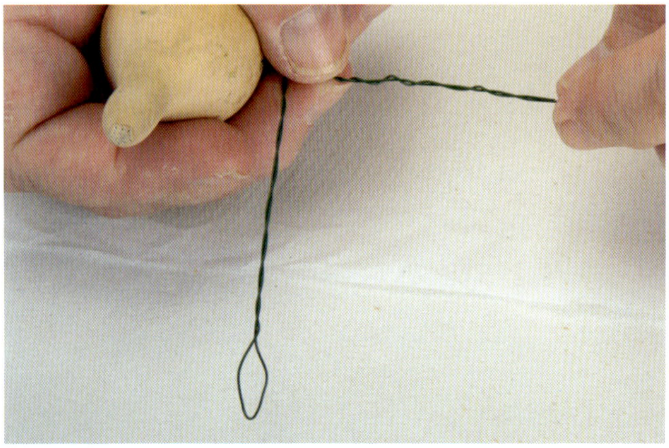

Twist the now-shorter wire with the longer wire to make a spine.

If the head seems loose, use needlenose pliers to give the wire at the back of the head a twist.

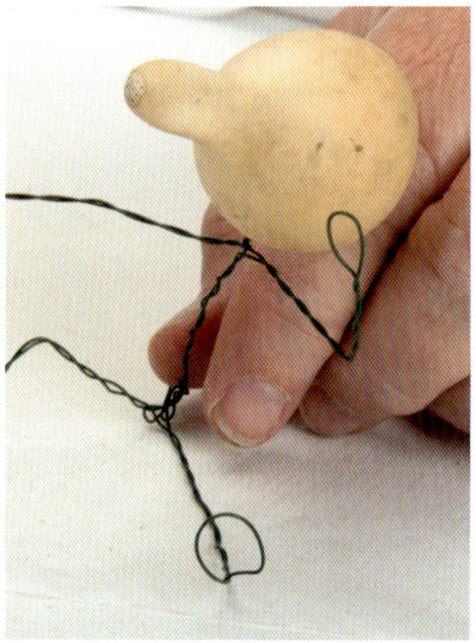

Wrap and tuck any leftover wire ends around the hip area.

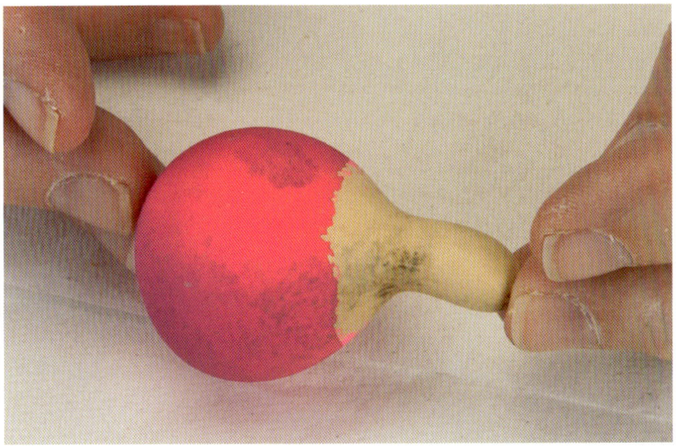

Spinner gourds are also good for birds too. To make a flamingo, begin with a spinner gourd for the head. Paint most of it pink, leaving the stem end unpainted for the nose.

FLAMINGO

Paint the face area white. This will curve like it's been stretched in a wide arc from one ear to another.

Paint the stem end, which will be the nose, black.

Add dots for eyes.

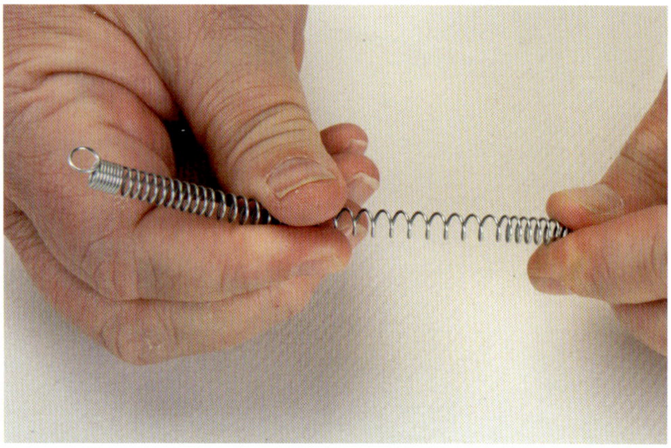

For the neck, stretch a small spring. (I buy these at a local hardware store.)

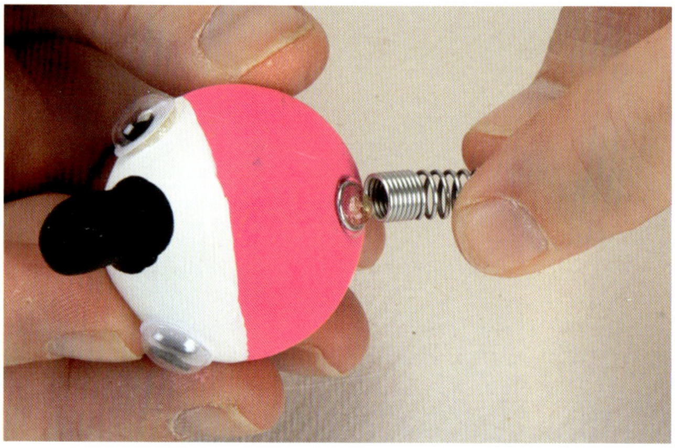

Hot-glue one end of the spring to the back of the head. Be sure the dot of glue is big enough to get caught up into the first couple of spirals of the spring.

Switch to an egg gourd for the bird's body. Paint it pink and drill a hole in one side to fit a dowel.

Paint a dowel with the diameter as the hole, and position it into the hole with glue.

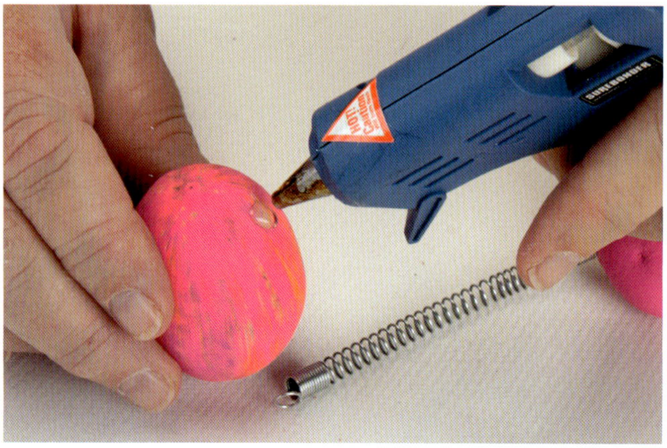

Hot-glue a spot where the neck with connect.

Quickly position the spring neck before the glue cools, so the glue grabs the spiral edges of the spring.

Drill small holes for wing and tail feathers.

Insert feathers with glue. I use white glue for this since the feathers won't fall out before it dries.

Add a top knot feather to the head.

Drill a hole into a wood base as a stand for the bird.

Bits of scrap can be shaped into feathers with pliers and painted pink . . .

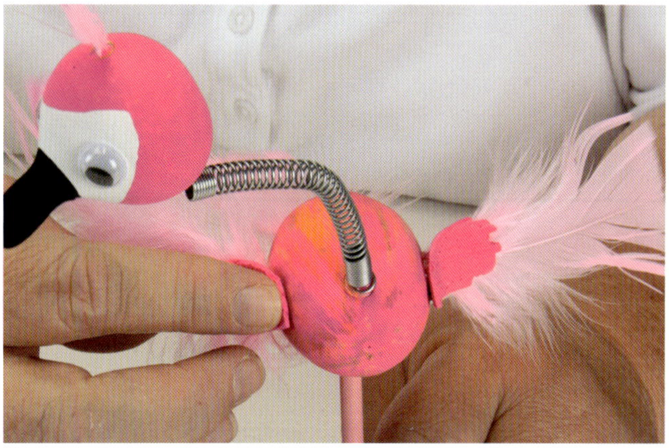

. . . for extra wing additions.

CHICKS

Another use for spinner gourds would be as part of an egg gourd chick project. Paint an egg gourd yellow and add black dots for eyes.

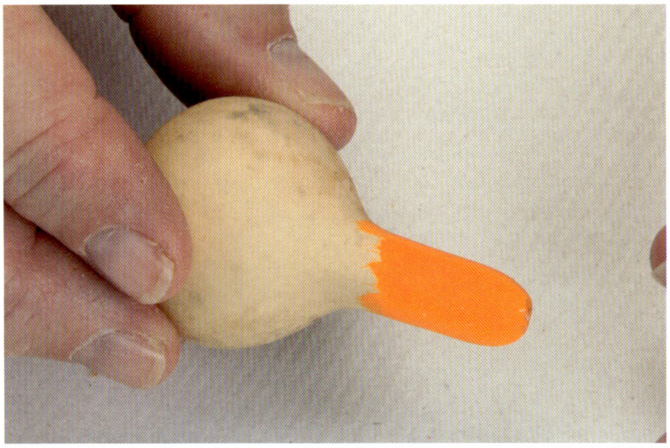

Paint the stem end of a spinner gourd orange for a beak.

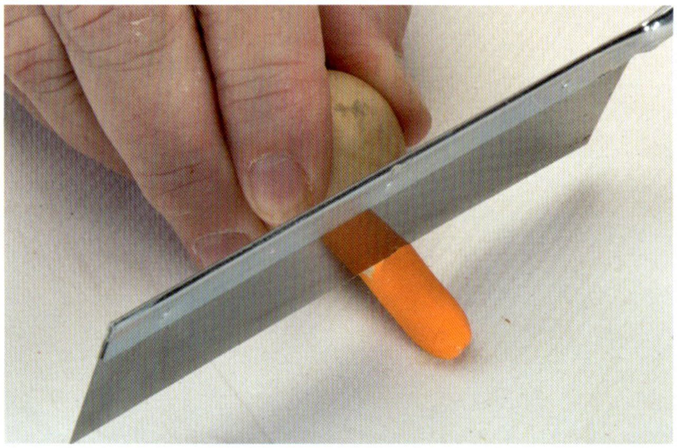

Cut off the beak.

Glue the beak into place.

For feet, start with a coated wire. (Dollar Tree offers packages of black- and red-coated wire—so nothing pricey.)

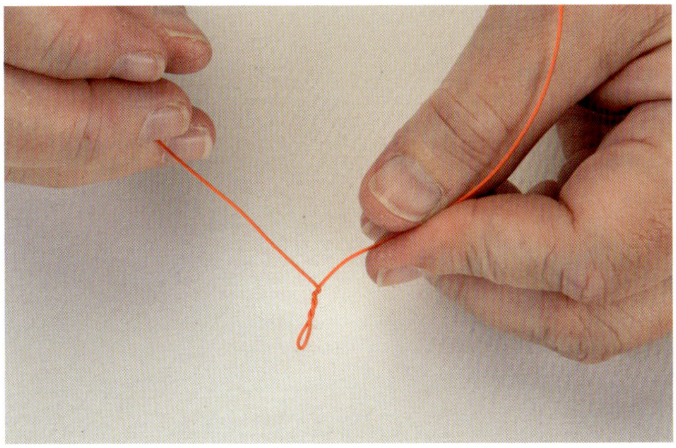

Make a small loop in the center, and twist it to make a toe.

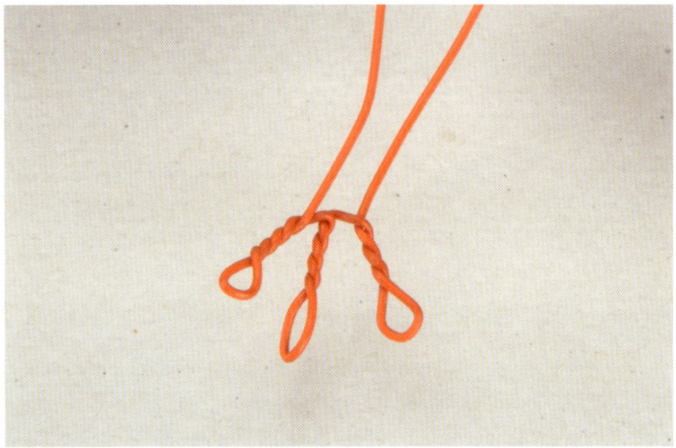

Right next to the toe, on either side, make two more toes.

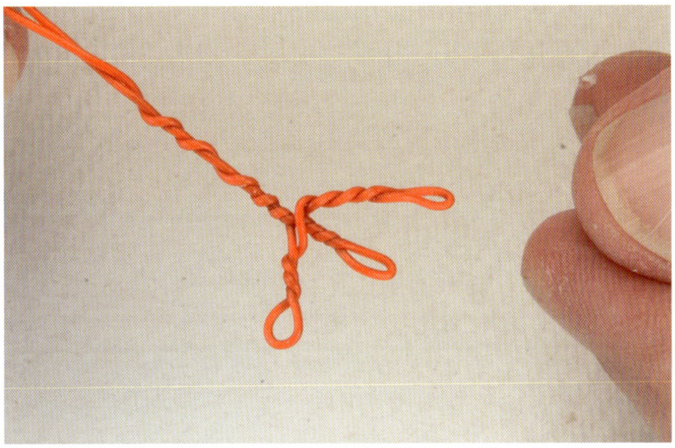

Twist the wire ends together for the leg.

Drill holes at the bottom of the egg gourd for the legs.

Hot-glue the legs into the holes.

Add a feather or loops of yarn to the top of the chick, for character.

MOVING TOYS

The history of toys, especially moving toys, is the history of mankind, the "progress of humans" (Gorman 1985). Early Mayan and Aztec archeological remains indicate that children played with wheeled carts made to look like animal bodies. The hobby horse was a popular childhood toy available from peddlers at medieval fairs, which was nothing more than an animal head on a stick that a child would straddle to mimic the knights and soldiers on parade. In fact, moving toys, which can be instructive or imitative, may have begun as experiments with physical properties of gravity, balance, magnetism, etc. (McMahon 2014). An example would be tops, originally from Japan but evidenced in all the early civilizations (Gorman 1985). Tops would have been fun to play with but would have also taught a child about speed and the phenomenon of persistent vision when colors and lines blur into one image as speed increases (Provenzo and Provenzo 1979). Knowledge of gravity and balance would have improved as a child learned to swing a tethered ball into a cup or to delicately place a skyhook on a shelf.

Moving toys as imitative devices (McMahon 2014) would have been a way to prepare small children for "cultural competence" (Bower 2018a) and to prepare for adulthood to test the waters, so to speak. Historically, sewing skills were learned when making clothes for homemade dolls, and items from nature were employed for pretend household activities, such as using acorn tops as plates for tea parties (Bledsoe 2002). Since early toys were made with commonly accessed materials such as wood or corn husks and reflected the environment and cultural traditions of the area where the toy was made and used (McMahon 2014), it is only small leap to think that hard-shelled gourds would have been used instead of, or in addition to, those materials. Let's make some simple moving toys with gourds to teach dexterity, mimic adult life, and demonstrate scientific discovery.

Exploring Physical Dexterity

As Helen Bledsoe (2002) describes in her article "Children in Colonial America Played with Homemade Toys," physical dexterity was and still is a skill that babies and small children develop while playing with toys, especially a push toy. Learning to walk is easier when babies play with long-handled push toys, since the handle functions as a balancing stick as the baby walks forward. Once the walking skill was achieved, a small child played with pull toys or even stick horses (Bledsoe 2002) as they walked faster and even ran.

DUCK PUSH TOY

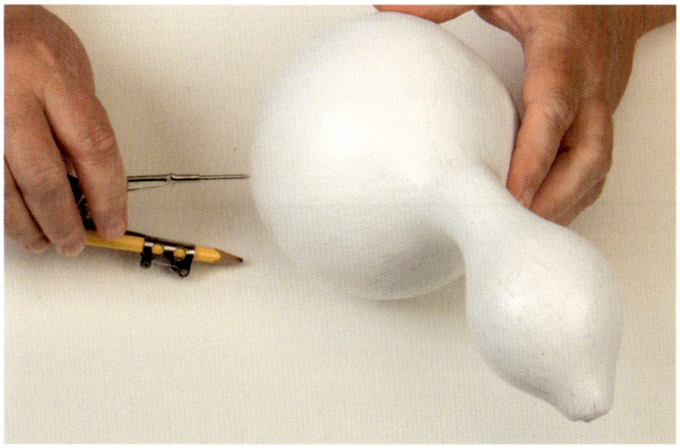

First, to find out how big the wheels need to be, measuring from the fattest part of the gourd belly to a flat surface.

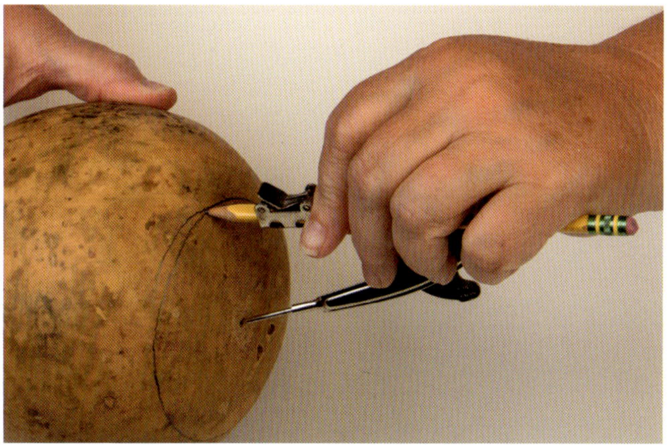

Use the measurement to draw a bigger circle on the flat bottom of two gourds to make two wheels. Note: the bigger circle lifts the gourd off the floor.

Use a mini jigsaw or handsaw to cut out the circles.

Drill a hole in the center of the circle to match the diameter of the wooden dowel being used for the axle, OR drill the hole a little off-center for a push toy that waddles lopsidedly.

Paint the circles white, and on each circle cut a slit from the edge toward the center with a handsaw.

Thread a birdhouse hole scrap and a circle (interior walls facing each other) onto the wooden dowel to align the holes.

Use dots of Super Glue Gel to attach the birdhouse hole to the wheel circle. Do this to both wheel units but don't get glue on the dowel.

Find the widest part of the duck belly and drill two holes, one on each side, for the wooded dowel that will be the axle for the wheels.

Position one of the wheel units at one end of the wooden dowel, and fix into place by putting a couple of drops of glue on the dowel and sliding the wheel unit over the glue.

After threading the axle through the body holes and positioning the other wheel unit, put glue on the dowel as you did earlier and slide the second wheel unit over the glue.

Trim off the excess dowel with a small saw and sand smooth. You can paint the nub white to match if you like.

Cut feet-shaped flaps from some leather to fit into the slits made in each wheel. Be creative—if you don't have leather, use plastic cutting boards or sheets of foam. The goal is to have something that is pliable enough to move with the wheel and still flap against the ground for a satisfying noise as the wheel rotates.

To make the flapping sound louder, add weight to the toe end of the feet. Here I cut and attach an additional layer of leather to add weight. Let glue dry.

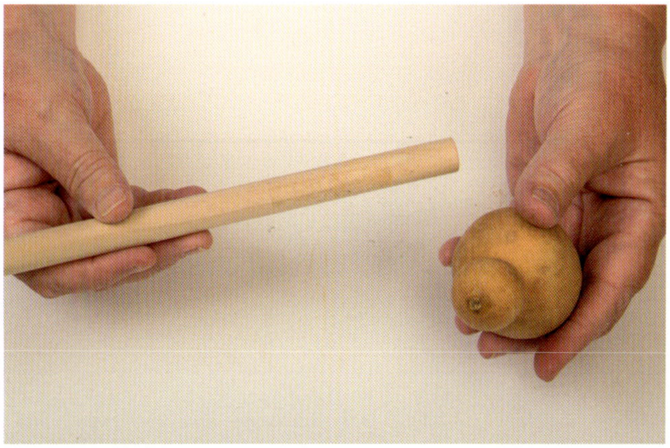

For the push toy handle, I use a ¾" wooden dowel and a mini bottleneck gourd.

Make a hole to fit the dowel snugly. Make sure the narrowed part of the gourd is wide enough for the dowel to pass through and reach the other end.

Remove the dowel far enough to put glue on it before sliding it back into the gourd to attach.

Make a similar hole on the backside of the duck body for a snug fit for the other end of the dowel. Insert small scraps of leather to fill in the gaps between the dowel and the hole, as needed, then glue into place for a tight-fitting hole.

Then glue feet flaps into the wheel slits.

Paint a duck face, following the flamingo face procedure but with orange paint. Add embellishments as desired. Note: Embellishments that swing and move as the duck is pushed forward are a bonus. Gluing pieces of leather to the wheel edges add to the bumping and jiggling impression.

STICK PONY

I start with a squat penguin or similarly shaped gourd, a tiki torch, a small gourd, ribbon, binder rings, and some upholstery edging. Be creative—again, this is the process I use for making a stick pony; use what you have on hand, and remember that no two will be alike!

Cut the tiki torch off the bamboo stick for the pony stick.

Using tape, pencil a centerline at the bottom of the gourd, going from one side to the other. The bamboo will be inserted along this line from the bottom (neck area) to the top (ears area).

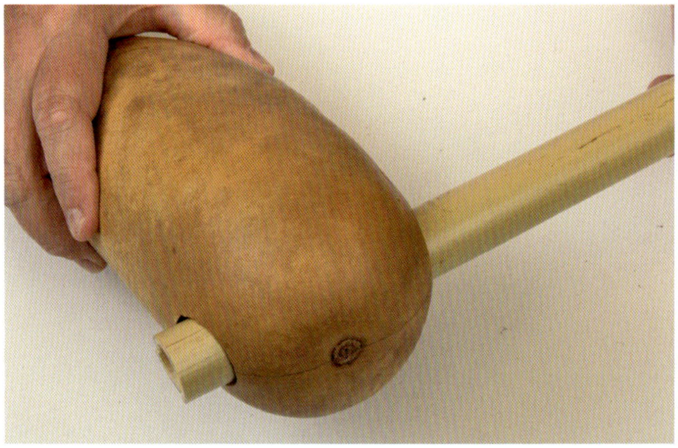

Drill holes and enlarge them enough to allow the bamboo to be inserted, which will not be perfect, but get as close as possible.

To each side of the hole used for the top of the head, drill additional holes for the earholes.

Cut oval shapes from scrap leather or foam sheets.

Glue into the earholes.

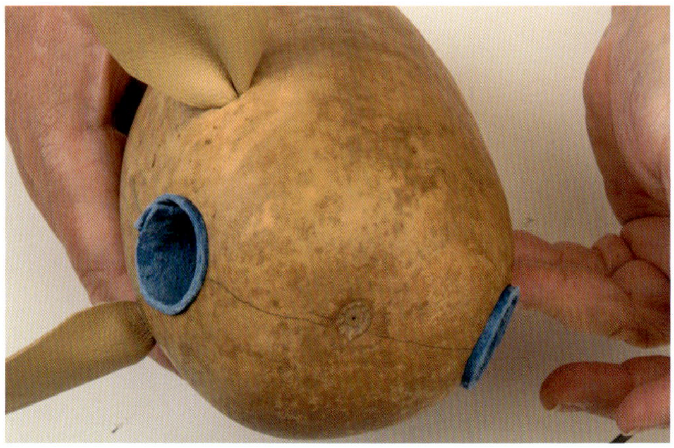

Glue a strip of leather to the inside of each hole for the bamboo, and let dry. This is done to give the bamboo a snug fit and a little more surface area for attachment for support.

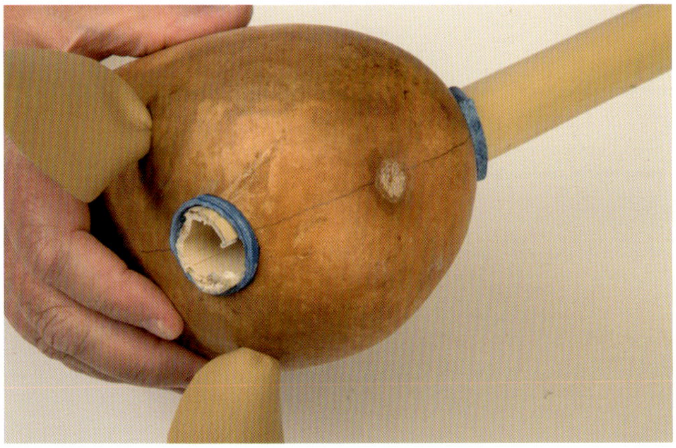

After pushing the bamboo through to test the fit, back the bamboo out enough to liberally apply glue to the hole, and push the bamboo back into place.

To add a small gourd at the other end of the bamboo as a finishing detail, make a hole, enlarge it, and glue the end of the bamboo into place, using leather if needed.

While the bamboo stick is drying into position, use ribbon and binder rings to make a harness. Measure and cut two pieces of ribbon for over and under the nose.

Bring the edge of the two ribbons through a binder ring, fold back, and hot-glue the overlap to hold it in place.

Use pushpins to hold it in place (wrong side out) on the bridge of the horse's nose while attaching the other binder ring to the opposite side. Pull the upper ribbon through the binder ring, fold back, and hot-glue into place.

Do the same with the lower ribbon.

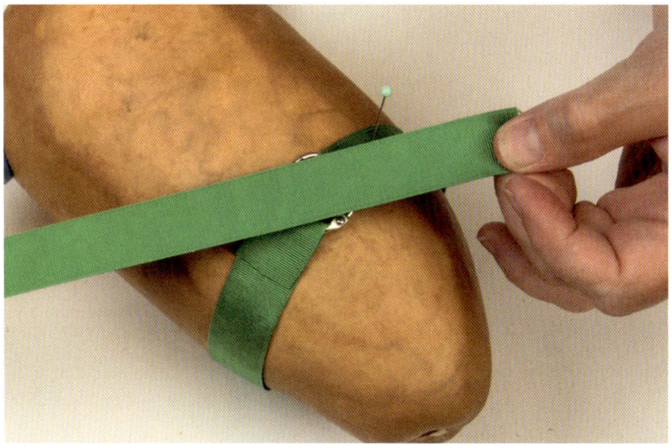

Cut two longer ribbons for reins that will reach from the binder rings to the backside of the bamboo stick, and tie together at one end.

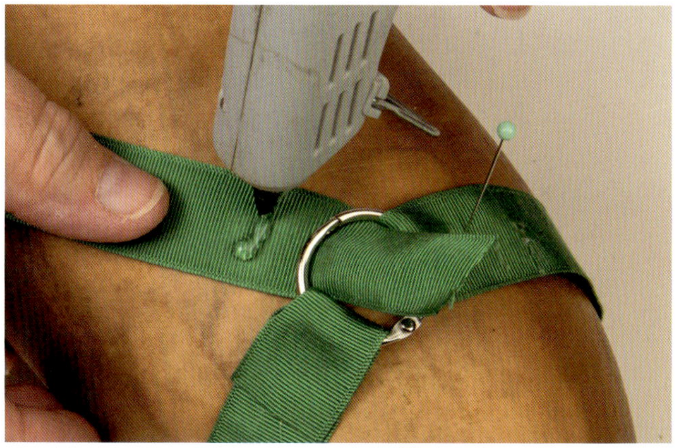

Put the ends through the rings, fold back, and hot-glue as with the other ribbons.

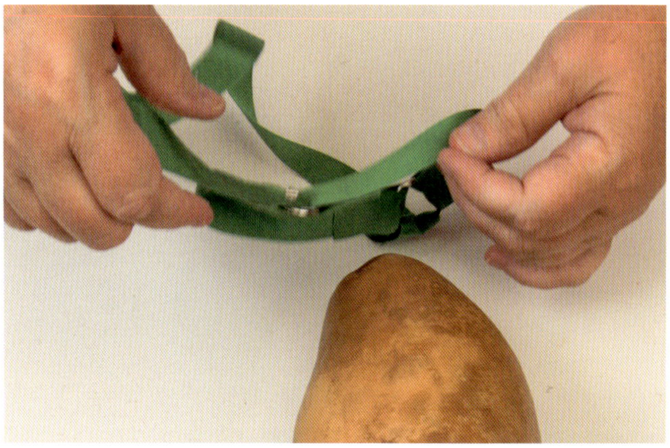

Take out the pushpins, turn the "harness" inside out, and put back on the horse head so the folded parts do not show.

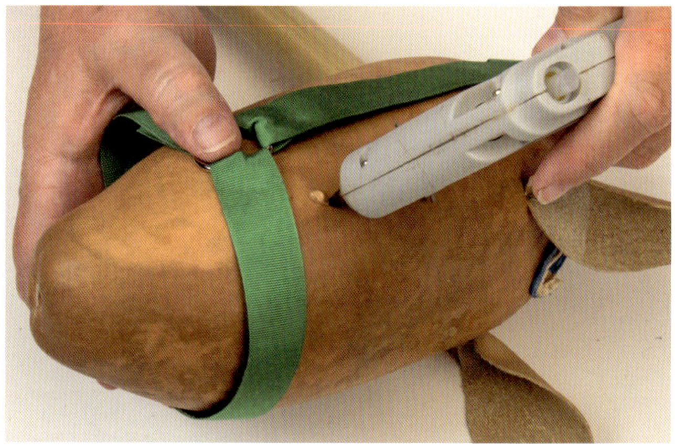

Hot-glue the folded area of the upper ribbon to the bridge of the horse's nose.

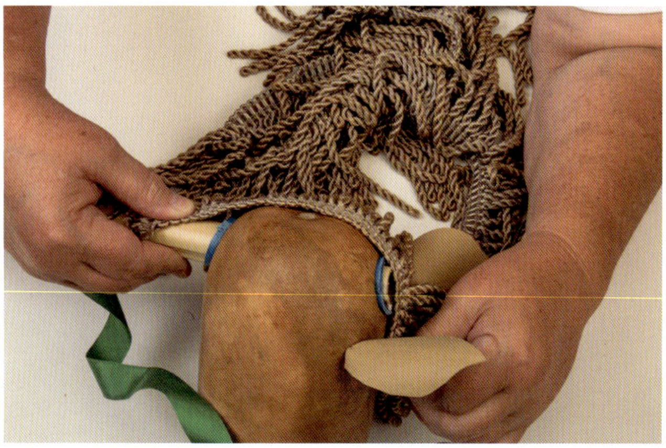

On to the mane! The easiest thing to do is use fringed upholstery edge. Cut two pieces several inches longer than the pencil line you made on the gourd at the beginning.

As a side note: if you don't have upholstery fringe, make your own fringe by tying yarn or strings onto a wide ribbon. It takes longer but, again, use what you have!

Hot-glue the two together so the fringe makes a single line of mane hair.

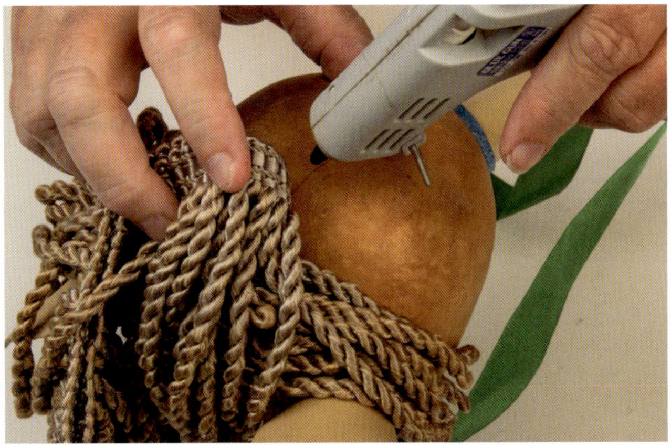

Flatten the base of the fringe on the gourd and hot-glue it along the pencil line. The opposite end is trimmed, folded under itself, and hot-glued to where the bamboo enters the gourd.

Eyes come in many sizes now and can be hot-glued onto the horse head if you don't want to paint them.

JUMP ROPE

Another old way of using a toy as physical play and fitness is a jumping rope! Early jump ropes recorded as playthings consisted of vines and flexible pieces of bamboo (Lee 2018). In the United States, children played jump rope as a game in the inner cities because it required only a rope and could engage many jumpers at once. Although jumping rope migrated from street game to the fitness arena, it encourages physical dexterity whether for a child or an adult.

Handles for a jump rope can be made from banana gourds, heads of swan gourds, or elongated miniature bottleneck gourds. Hands must encircle the handles for a good grip, and the rope entry holes need to withstand wear.

Gut the ends to remove pith and dust.

Drill a hole in the end of each gourd, through which the rope or cord will pass, and use E6000 to secure ¼" eyelets into the holes. These used to be called grommets, but the packages I get now say "large eyelets" on them.

Cut enough rope or cord so it's about the height of the person jumping plus 3 feet. There are several mathematical formulas for measuring how long the rope should be, but this is the one I use. Thread one end of the rope through the handle, so the opposite end can be knotted and pulled inside the handle to be hidden.

The other side will need to be threaded in the opposite direction, since the knot will be the opposite end of the rope.

You can fancy up the handles by decorating the gourd ends first or adding beads to the ends of the rope knots so they dangle outside the handle.

PRACTICING CULTURAL ROLES

Makeshift playthings produced to delight or be helpful seem to be better for learning real tasks than are imaginary objects or fantasy (Bower 2018b). As stated earlier, easily accessible pieces of wood and bits of cloth would have been used to improvise playthings such as dolls for learning tea party manners, or knights for learning heroism in mock battles. In traditional communities, children play with real tools or reproductions of real tools in order to enact adult situations in preparation for growing up to do those tasks for themselves (Bower 2018b). Considering this, it would seem plausible that a human figure made with moving joints would be more lifelike than one without them.

Adding movement to a gourd human can be done with wire, string, and eye screws. There are reasons to use one over another, on the basis of what is available to use, how frequently the figure will be handled, and how varied the range of motion needs to be. Those decisions are the ones made as you create.

GOURD PEOPLE AND PARTS

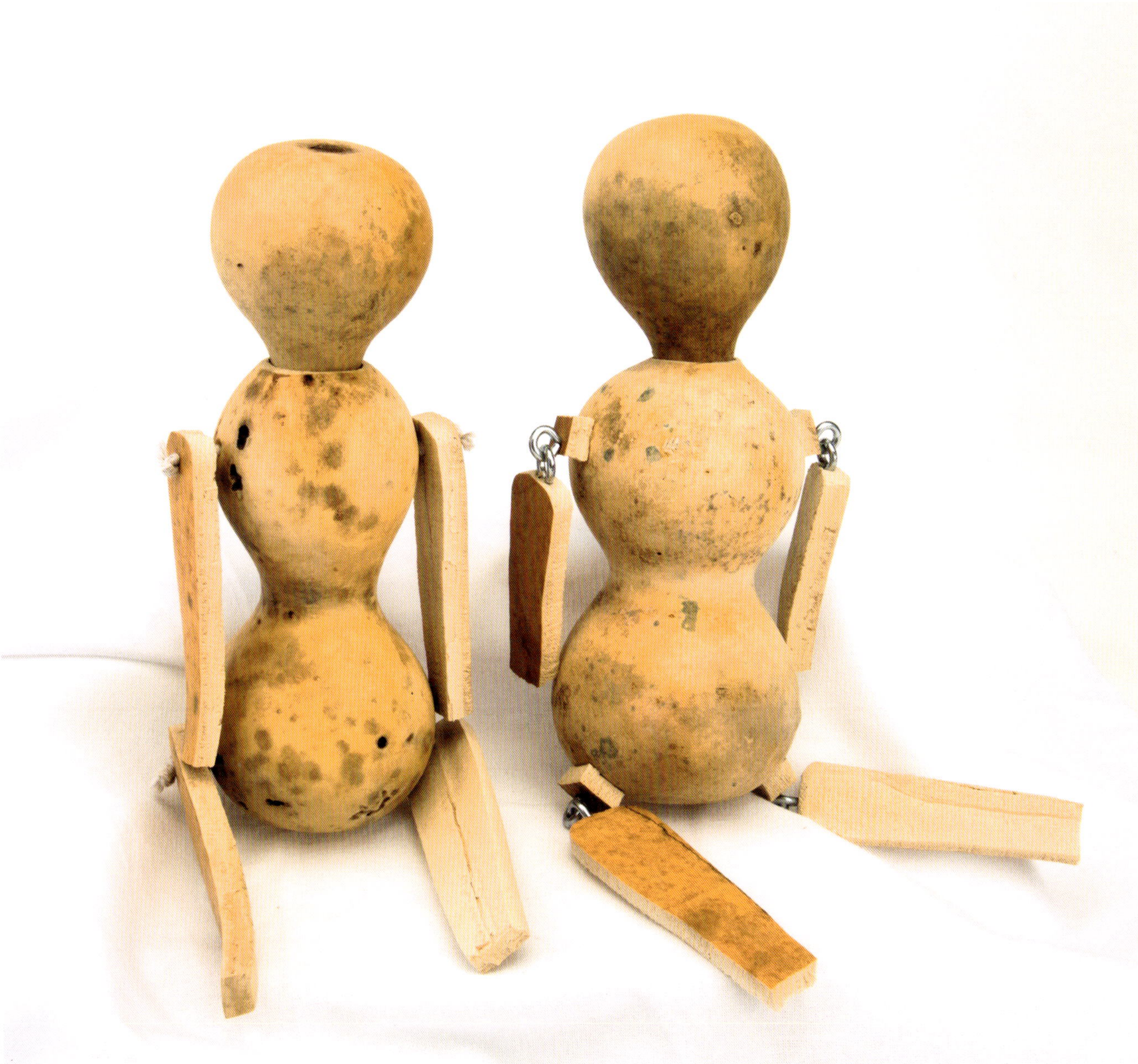

Gourd doll arms and legs can be made by cutting a gourd into strips. Begin with a gourd with relatively flatish sides, and pencil cut lines to look like stripes.

Use a handsaw or mini jigsaw to cut every other line. I have tried cutting every line and found the vibrations caused more trouble than the time I thought I was saving . . .

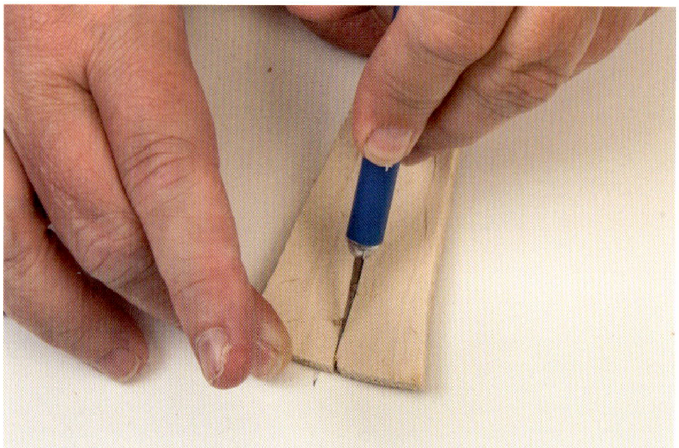

. . . so cut every other one to make broad stripes, then use an X-ACTO to score the backside of the pieces.

The pieces will snap apart along the scored line.

Smooth and round the edges as desired. I personally use Sandblaster sandpaper taped to a board to sand small pieces of gourd. Double-sided tape holds the paper in place, and Sandblaster does not clog readily, so it does not need to be changed frequently.

To begin a gourd person, choose a bottleneck gourd that seems to be body shaped.

Sand a hole at the top to insert a spinner gourd for a head.

For the arms and legs, drill holes for arms and legs into the fattest part of the bottleneck gourd's upper and lower bellies.

Drill a hole at one end of the arm and leg scraps.

Cut two wires long enough to extend a couple of inches beyond the arms and legs when threaded through them and the body at the same time.

Thread one wire through an arm on one side of the gourd's upper belly, through the belly to the other arm. There should be an equal amount of leftover wire on both sides.

Curl the wire at the shoulder joint and leg joint, so it flattens against the arm and leg. The pieces should be secure but still move when tilted one way or the other.

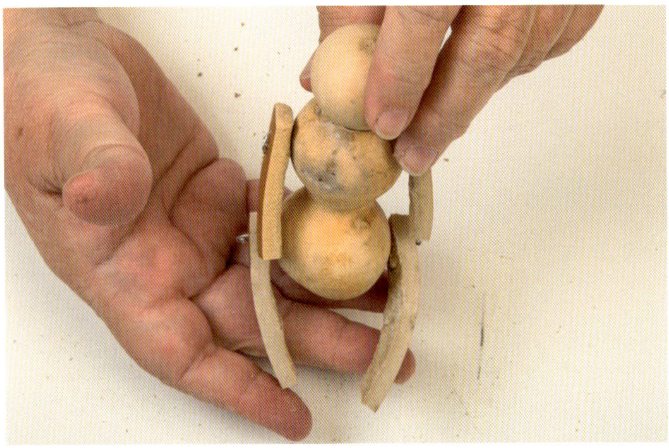

Do the same with the legs. Everything should swing around on the wires when moved.

This same movement can be made with string. Make the holes as done with the wire.

Eye screws are an option if you can find them small enough. Eye screws will need a support piece of gourd to keep them in place.

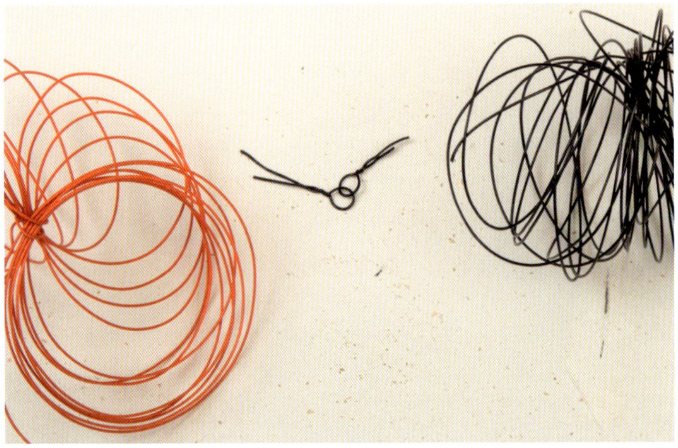

Making eye screws is easy when color wire is needed to complete a design. Begin with lengths of coated color wire.

Wrap one wire around a skewer or other cylinder-shaped object, and twist.

Loop another wire through the circle of the eye screw and, using the skewer, make another eye screw. This makes a couplet.

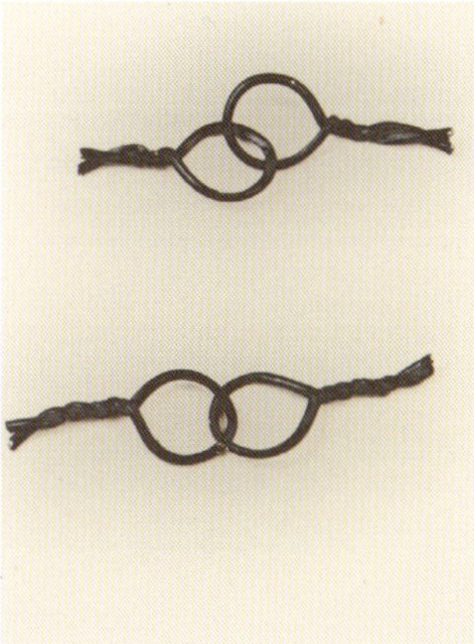

Trim the ends to about ½".

Drill a small hole into the ends of two scraps.

Put glue into the hole of one scrap, and stick one end of the couplet into it.

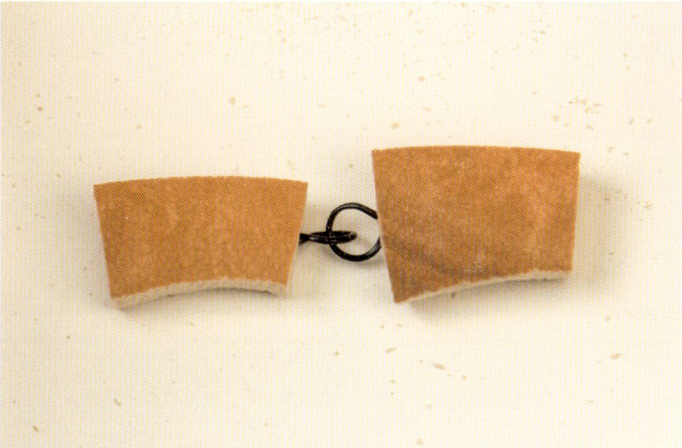

Do the same for the other scrap and let dry. If making arms or legs with multiple joints, line up the scraps so all the couplets can be done at one time.

In the fish shelf-sitter, I used V-shaped files to produce the fish shape. The black-coated wire was chosen to mimic the black woodburned lines.

In the cow shelf-sitter, red-coated wire was used to accent the black-and-white cow colors. A spinner gourd and spinner gourd tips were used to make the udder bag.

LEARNING THE LAWS OF NATURE

All humans, especially children, are curious and want to know cause and effect in order to understand the world around them. This type of inquiry has an evolutionary purpose, since curiosity leads people to answer questions, thereby reducing fear and causing changes in behavior (Wernick 2017). As the novelties for the wealthy became more complicated, "art and science merged" (Gorman 1985). Can you imagine how a scientific principle used as a basis to make a wealthy person's entertainment could be translated into a homemade folk toy, using common materials? Even today, with all the electronic devices at our fingertips, simple toys made as updated versions of colonial toys, without batteries or electronics, are popular (Ballman 1992). Gourds can be used to reproduce some of the quirky and oddly named toys to demonstrate science. Let's get scientific!

SPEED-SPINNER GOURDS

A spinner gourd is a small, top-like gourd, so named because it spins. The Australian Museum has documented a top made from a gourd, one of only six surviving examples of playthings used by men in the late 1800s. In the Cairns region, indigenous men held contests to see whose top would spin the longest. Remnants of color suggest that the men may have decorated their gourds (Wheeler 2012). Painting a spinner gourd on different sides and spinning would demonstrates how speed affects vision.

Here are a dirty and a cleaned spinner gourd.

This spinner gourd is painted using craft paints. Sitting still, the images are clear.

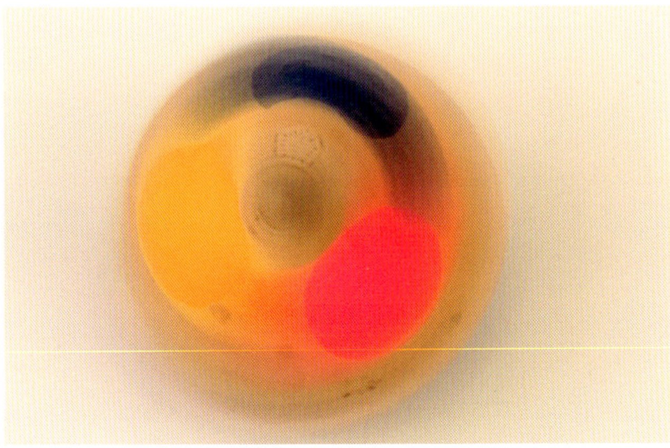

However, spinning the spinner produces the optical illusion so entrancing to kiddos and adults alike!

SPEED—THAUMATROPE

An old toy demonstrating the principle of speed affecting vision is the thaumatrope, which is a spinning disk with an image on both sides of the disk. It is supposed to have been the entry into cinematics (Provenzo and Provenzo 1979). It shows how the phenomenon of persistent vision works: when an image hits the retina of the eye, it remains for a faction of a second, blurring with other images that come faster than the retina can regain stasis or equilibrium. As the thaumatrope is spun with the strings attached to the sides of the disks, the front and back images are blended into one. Speed messes with what the eye sees!

To make a thaumatrope, use a piece of gourd scrap, and drill holes into each side. Thread a string through the holes.

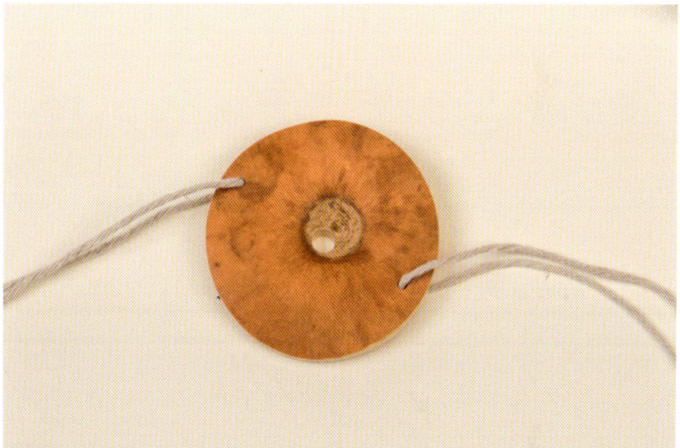

Then tie a string through each hole.

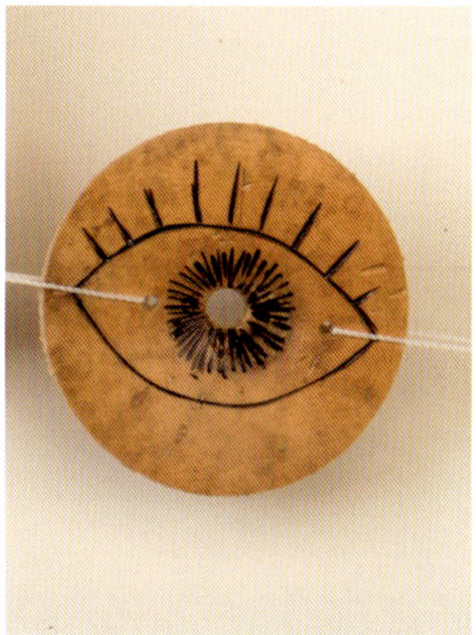

Spinning movement and persistent vision make two images blend. This thaumatrope has an eye on one side

. . . and eyelashes on the other.

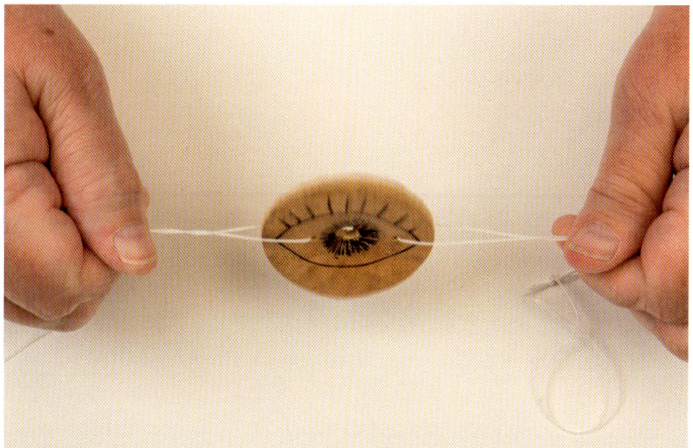

When spun, the eye and eyelashes combine.

The classic images for this traditional toy are a bird and a cage, where the bird is on one side . . .

. . . and the cage is on the other. Twist the strings with your fingers, or swing around to tighten the strings, so when pulled the tension is released.

Use online free clip art for your thaumatrope—fireflies and a jar (for fireflies in a jar) or a heart and a hand (for a hand holding a heart). This one has a jar and . . .

. . . three "Xs" to symbolize moonshine.

SPEED—FLYING FISH

Another lesson involving speed also speaks to centrifugal force: the faster a tethered object spins around a center, the higher it flies. This works with anything tied to a string and spun in circles, even if it is only held by a person's hand while spinning. It also explains why, when the string is released, the tethered object flies off in a straight line from the point where it left the spinning circle of energy! The faster the spinning, the more force the object has, and therefore the higher it flies or the farther it flies away if released!

Using a fish we made earlier, drill a hole at the nose end of the gourd. Tie a knot at the end of 1 yard of string or twine. and use a sharp tool to jam the knot into the gourd through the hole.

Add another drop or two of white glue into the hole. Let dry.

The fish can be swung around with your hand as it, or you can make a twirling stick by tying the end of string around the narrow waist of a mini bottleneck gourd. Leave it loose enough to be able to slide around the waist easily but not slip over the upper or lower bellies of the gourd.

Drill a hole at the end of the mini gourd, big enough so a dowel can be inserted and extend all the way through to the opposite end. I usually pull out the dowel a little to put white glue on it and then push it back into the gourd.

Now the fish can be swung above and around far above your head.

SPEED—WHIMMYDIDDLE

Whimmydiddles and flipperdingers are two classic toys played with by children in the Appalachian hills (Tabler 2015). Whimmydiddle. Don't you just love this word? It's fun to say, but not as much fun as using the other terms for it: voodoo stick, gee haw stick, hooey stick. All these terms refer to a centuries-old toy used when asking questions. By dragging another stick over the grooves cut into the whimmydiddle, elliptical vibrations make the whirligig at the end spin one way or the other to indicate answers. Of the other terms for a whimmydiddle (voodoo stick, hooey stick, gee haw stick), voodoo suggests magic, hooey is defined as nonsense and rubbish, and gee haw indicated two traditional verbal directions for driving horses or oxen: *gee* for going right and *haw* for going left. Will Hines, a whimmydiddle champion, explains that the gee haw works by using finger pressure against one side or the other to change the speed of vibration on that side, which makes the whirligig spin right or left (Simmons 2011). I can make the whirligig spin, but haven't mastered the gee or haw of it yet, so I take all the answers to my questions to be yes!

The parts for the whimmydiddle include a long, straight handle from a dipper gourd, a flat gourd scrap for the whirligig, and a piece of coat hanger half as long as the handle. Begin by gutting the gourd handle.

Drill a hole into the end of the gourd handle and through the whirligig scrap to make loose holes for the coat hanger wire.

Curl the end of the coat hanger wire (that is half as long as the gourd handle you are using) so the whirligig is kept in place but is not slowed down with contact.

Use a handsaw to make V-shaped cuts into the handle along the length of one side. The point here is to make enough sharp ridges that will build up energy to produce vibrations when rubbed with a stick.

Insert coat hanger wire into the hole at the end.

Vigorously rub across the ridges, back and forth, with a stick—in this case I used another gourd handle. By subtly touching the gourd handle on one side or the other as you rub the ridges with the stick, the whirligig will twirl one direction or the other—gee or haw.

GRAVITY—FLIPPERDINGERS

Flipperdingers, on the other hand, are based on gravity. A flipperdinger is a hollow tube that one blows through to use air pressure to levitate a small ball or pompom at the opposite end (Tabler 2015). Long handles from a dipper gourd seem a natural for this. They are hollow and can be prepared with an air hole, upon which a lightweight pompom can sit. As a person blows through the hollow tube, air pressure through the hole makes the pompom rise through a wire ring and fall back into position. Controlling the air blowing through the hole is the trick! Sometimes there is a small wire hook wrapped around the pompom, so after rising through the ring, it can be maneuvered to hook onto the ring. I'm still trying to control the air flow to get a straight up-and-down movement!

This is what I do in the garage for silly entertainment. I blow pompoms through a wire ring at the end of a dipper gourd's long handle . . . the gourder's version of a flipperdinger.

You can too. Begin with a 9"–10" piece of handle from a dipper gourd and a couple of spinner gourds.

First, gut the handle of pith and seeds. I use a tire pump to blow out small bits and dust. Also, I swish the interior with an acrylic floor polish to capture any further dust from releasing.

Glue a spinner gourd into one end as an air block.

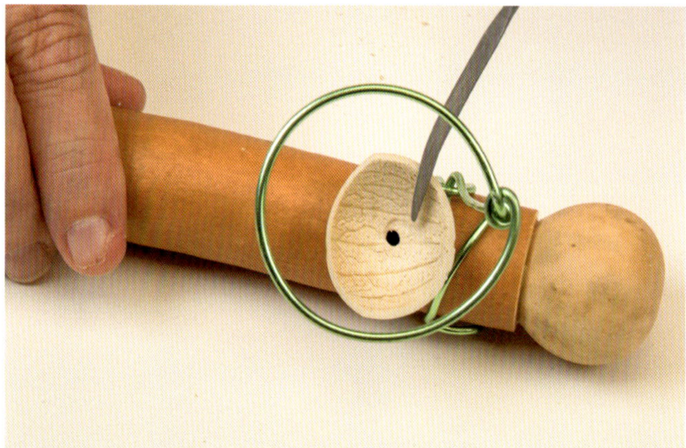

Toward the end of the handle with the air block, drill a 1⁄8"–3⁄16" blow hole through a piece of spinner gourd and the gourd handle. Note: a bigger hole will require a lot more lung capacity, so don't be overly generous. The spinner gourd scrap will serve as a catch cup. Use Super Glue Gel to attach it to the handle.

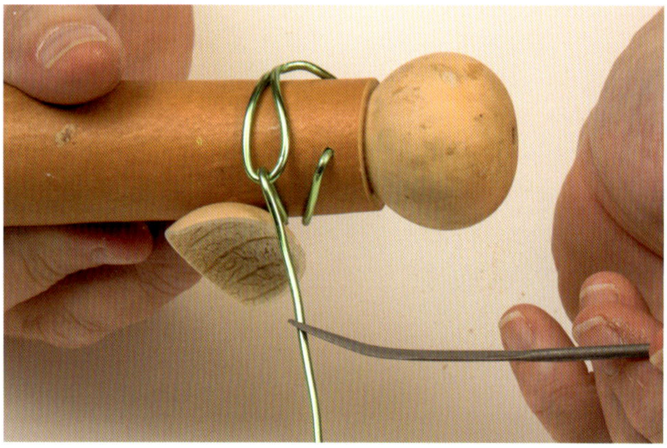

Drill a small hole between the catch cup and the air block at the end that is big enough to anchor the wire being used for the levitating ring. Make the ring of wire and bend it so it is positioned about 3" above the catch cup.

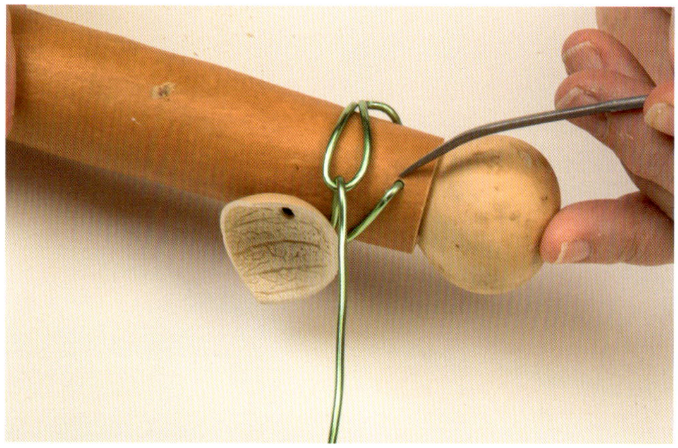

Wrap the wire around the handle and the base of the levitating ring, eventually pushing the end of the wire into the small hole made earlier.

Now you are ready to learn breath control to levitate the sphere through the ring. A master at this game can manage to levitate the sphere up through the ring and back down again . . . but that's not me.

*Note—the handles do not have to be straight.

GRAVITY—BALL TOSS

Ball tosses are natural moving toys! A ball is tethered to a cup of some sort, and by swinging it up and aligning the ball to the cup, it can drop straight down into the cup. Not only does the child learn eye-hand coordination but discovers gravity. The bigger the ball, the longer it takes to swing it up and the faster it falls. Playing outside probably incorporated the changes wind can have on a falling object as well. All good cause-and-effect lessons.

Using a cannonball gourd and the end of another gourd, drill a hole into each to accommodate a string.

Insert a knotted string into the cannonball gourd as was done with the fish for the flying-fish toy.

Add a drop of glue after the knot is inserted.

Put the other end of the string through a hole at the edge of the bottleneck top that was cleaned out as a cup. Make sure the hole is not too close to the edge in order to support the swinging cannonball. Tie the end.

GRAVITY—HOURGLASS

Hourglasses have been recorded since the 1300s, about the time that mechanical timepieces came about (Lienhard 1988), and would have been an interesting way to learn about gravity, since so many factors affect the gravity involved with falling sand: the angle of the container's wall, the size of the hole through which the sand moves, and sand erosion over time (Mills et al. 1996). As a science project, any one of these factors would be a discovery. Basically, the steeper the container wall is, the more gravity pulls on the particles to fall.

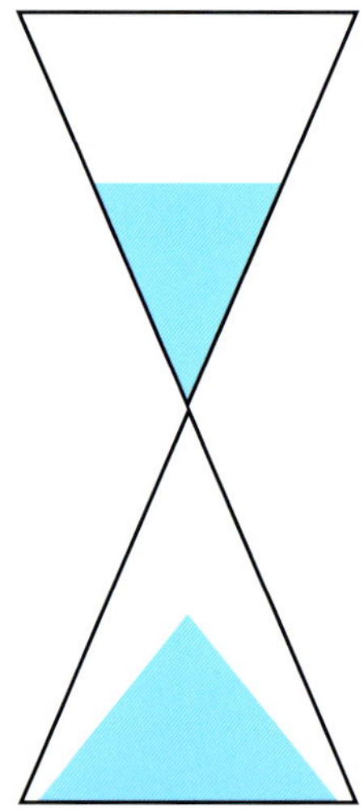

The more vertical the wall, the faster the particles fall. As the wall angle flattens, the particles slow or stop falling.

Prime example: I used round plastic ornament balls for one hourglass, and the particles do not empty completely on their own.

The particle-to-hole ratio also matters: the smaller the particles falling through the hole between the top and the bottom chambers, the faster they will move. Since I use scrap entry holes from birdhouse projects, I try to gauge the particle size of the sand or gravel I'm using to allow continuous flow through the hole made by the drill bit. Finally, as a heads up, the edges of the falling particles will erode over time with use. This phenomenon is not apparent immediately but will eventually change the accuracy of a timepiece.

Because gourds are opaque, the possibility of using them for an hourglass container is not practical. However, using gourd scraps in combination with transparent containers can make good demonstrations of angle and gravity. Although each hourglass is an individual creation, these basics will get you started.

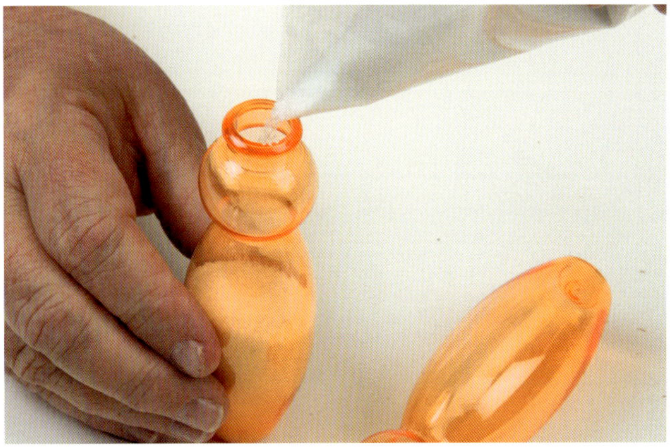

To connect two containers together, such as these hummingbird feeders, start by putting the particles in one container.

In a birdhouse hole scrap, sand away some of the material at the hole to make an angle.

Use E6000 on the rim of the container with the sand.

Place the scrap on top of the E6000 at the rim of the container and let dry.

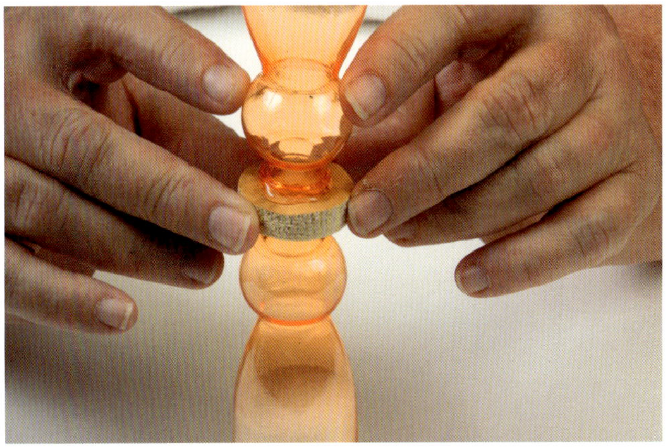

Put E6000 on the rim of the empty container and set it on top of the birdhouse hole unit. Let dry. Don't touch. Leave it undisturbed.

The gourd scraps made the leaves, as shown earlier in this book, a fork was bent for a hanger, and wire was twisted around the hourglass so it hangs on the fork. The whole gourd was made bottom heavy, with sand poured into it before the fork was anchored into place.

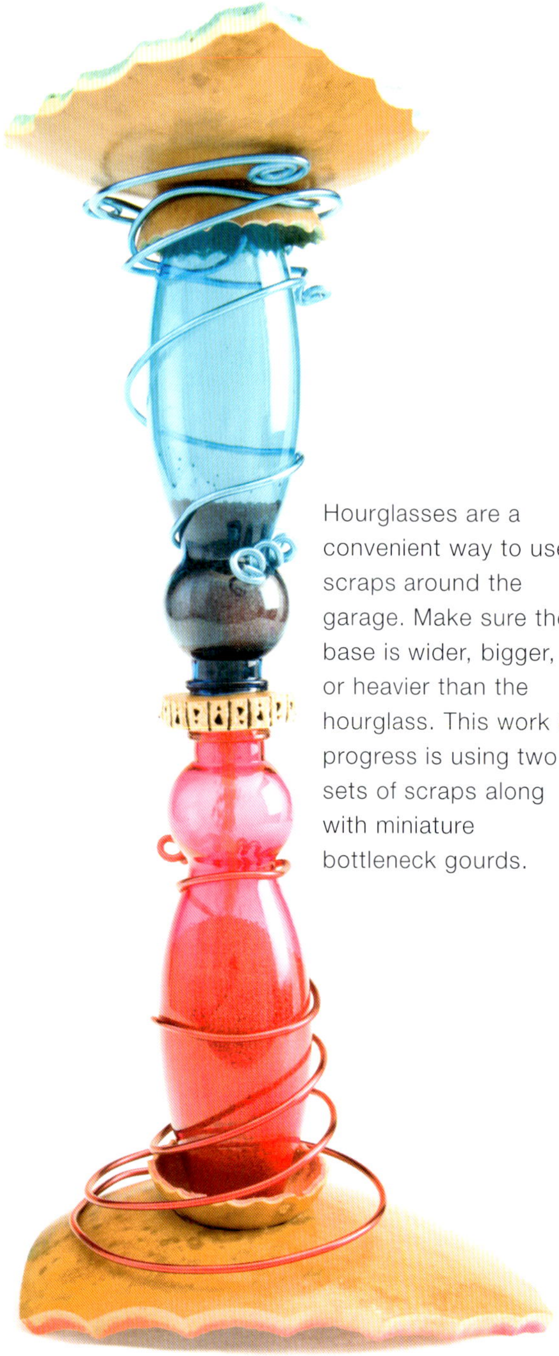

Hourglasses are a convenient way to use scraps around the garage. Make sure the base is wider, bigger, or heavier than the hourglass. This work in progress is using two sets of scraps along with miniature bottleneck gourds.

In this example, garage gourd scraps, weird stuff sitting on the work table, and wires were used.

GRAVITY—ACROBAT TOY

Forcing a shift of an object's weight adds movement due to gravity. In a video about an old folk toy, acrobat Rick Mayotte (2016) explains how the system of cross-fitting string makes movement happen, because the strings are stretched to untwist. When this is done, the figure's weight is flipped around willy-nilly. Adding weight to one end of the figure makes the action become a more controlled up-or-down movement.

Use two thick dowels about 1' long and a mini bottleneck gourd to make the frame. Drill a set of two holes about ½" apart at one end of the dowels, and at the other end of the dowels (image shows where the grip will be) drill holes through the dowels to fit a skewer.

Find the fattest part of the mini bottleneck gourd and drill similar hole on both sides to run the skewer through one dowel, the gourd, and the other dowel.

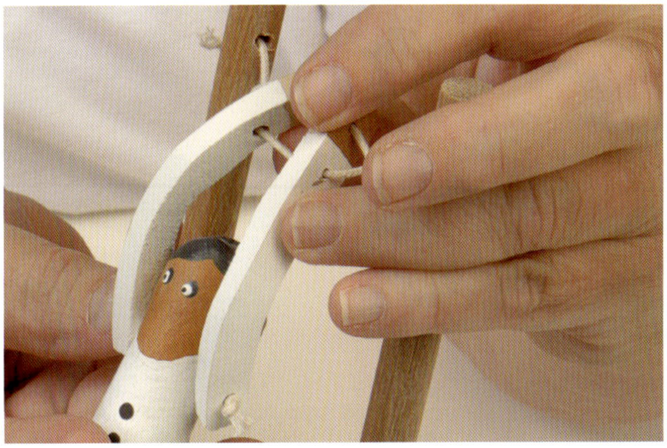

Make a man with string joints as shown earlier in the book. Make sure the body is narrow and that the arms extend well beyond the head. Make two holes at the end of each arm for the hands.

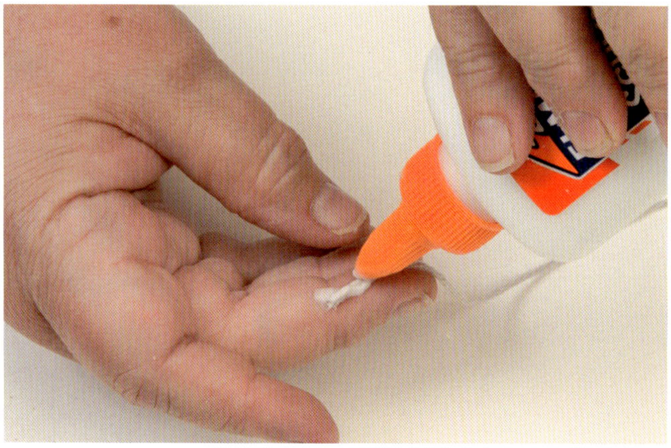

Cut about 2' of string and use glue to saturate the end of the string to make a natural needle. Let dry.

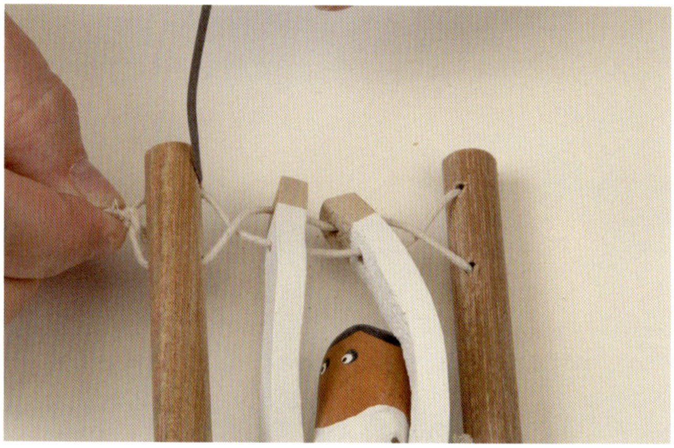

The threading is what makes this toy work. Take the hardened end of the string and go through the upper hole at the end of one of the dowels.

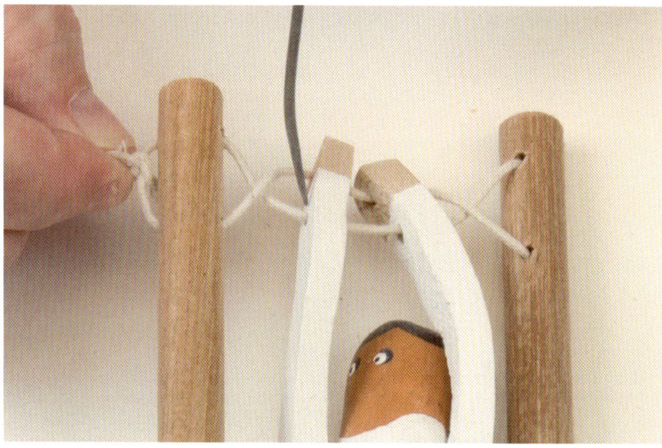

Go through the lower hole on the closest arm . . .

. . . and through the lower hole in the other arm.

Move to the upper hole on the opposite dowel.

Go to the lower hole on the same dowel . . .

. . . and then through the upper holes on both arms.

Go through the lower hole on the first dowel and tie a knot.

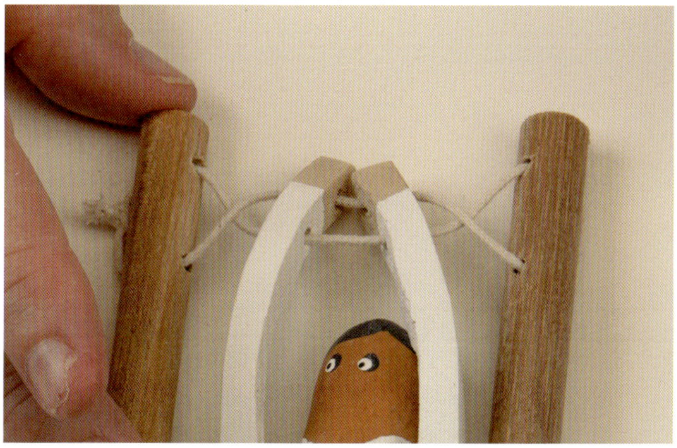

Because the crisscross of strings is above the center of gravity, squeezing the dowels apart to untwist the strings is what makes the flipping happen.

In this bee example, the crisscross of strings is below the center of gravity, so it produces a different motion. Instead of flipping up and over, the object in this toy just flips up and down.

GRAVITY—RACE CAR

The Boy Scouts of America have pinewood derby races each year, using blocks of wood, aerodynamics, and gravity. A considerable amount of time and scientific knowledge is combined for sleek appearance and a no-friction roll. Once the cars are built, they are lined up side by side on elevated tracks and released to roll toward a finish line. Gravity does the work. What if gourds were used instead of blocks of wood? Wouldn't they be lighter? And faster? These are good questions and certainly worthy of further exploration. For this book, let's make a race car!

To make this race car, I am using a UFO banana gourd project from the garage—it was layered with colors from one end toward the other end.

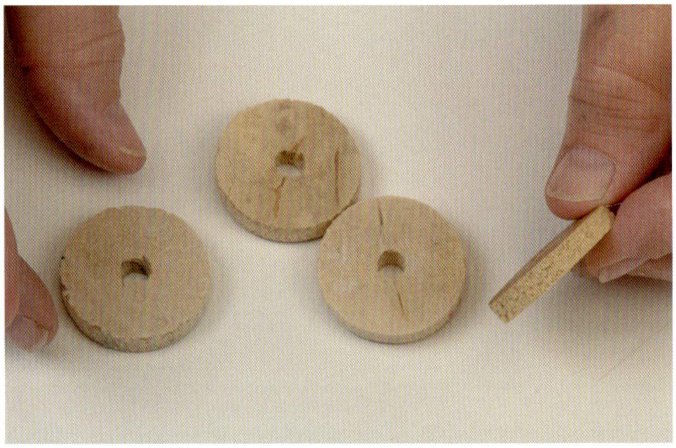

For the tires, sand the backside of the birdhouse hole scraps but don't sand the edges, because when painted, the rough edges will look like tire treads.

Paint the tires black and add silver paint to the center as hubcaps.

Drill holes for the dowels that will be used as wheel axles. The goal is to make sure the holes are parallel. A drill bit will usually go straight through a banana gourd from one side to the other.

Thread the dowels through the holes.

Adding a bead to each side of the axle will keep the wheel from rubbing the body of the car. The beads at the fatter end of the banana gourd will be smaller than the beads at the narrow end, since the tires at the narrow end have a greater chance of not clearing the car.

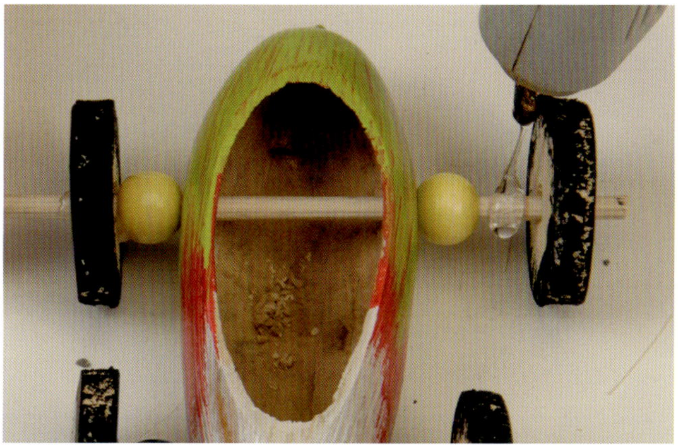

Slide the wheels onto the axles. Once you see that the wheels can rotate without meeting the body, hot-glue the wheels into position.

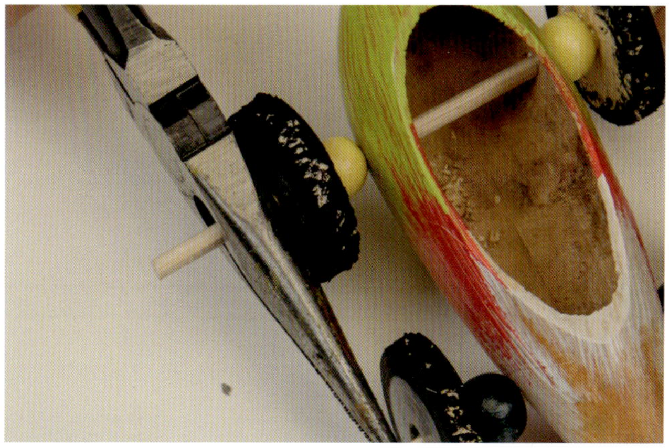

Trim off excess dowel.

GRAVITY—FLAMINGO FAMILY

From my own memories of childhood, springs provided motion in toys. Isaac Newton's laws of motion explained how spring rocking horses galloped, why Slinky meandered down the stairs by itself, and how bobblehead dogs nodded convincingly as my parent's car made its way down the highway. Bobblehead dolls, as shown in an earlier book, *Gourd Puppets and Dolls: A Do-It-Yourself Guide for Crafters* (2008), use springs to make a head wobble and bobble when tapped. The same action happens when strategically placing a spring-neck bird sculpture in the wind or on a jiggling surface, for never-ending movement as energy is transferred to the springs and released.

The spring-necked flamingo made earlier can be combined with a variety of other gourds to make an interesting bobbing display. In this case, one flamingo head is placed inside an egg gourd.

To make a broken egg gourd shell, use an X-ACTO knife to begin a crack.

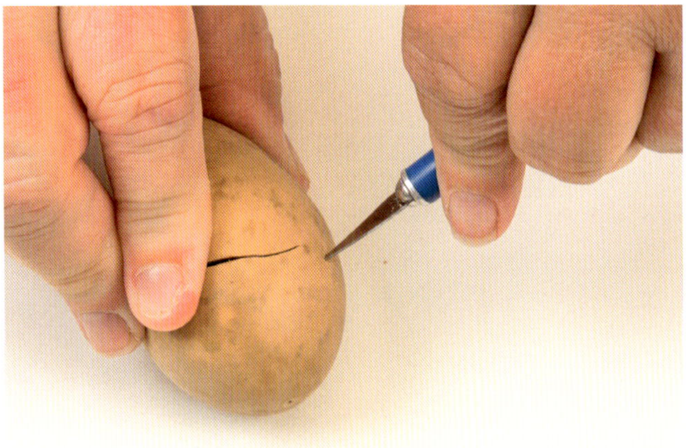

As the gourd cracks, reenter the X-ACTO in a different direction so the zigzag line breaks randomly around the belly of an egg gourd.

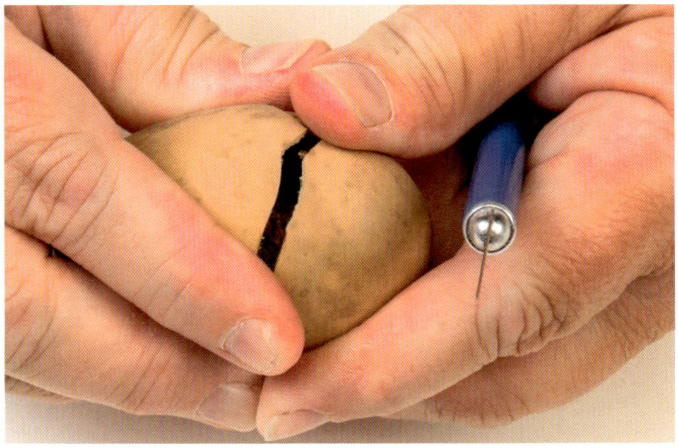

As the line breaks, keep directing the crack and open.

Paint white and put the head inside so the flamingo nose pokes out.

BALANCE—BALANCING BIRD

Balancing anything involves understanding the center of gravity. A balancing bird can be made a couple of ways. It can be cut from the side of a large gourd as one piece, making sure the wings protrude forward from the head, which is the center of gravity, so they balance with the body. It can also be done by attaching wings made of gourd scraps to the sides of a banana gourd. In this case, the same principle applies—the wings need to come forward to balance the body.

This is the template for a balancing bird. Notice how the wings extend far beyond the head to get a center of gravity. THAT'S the key.

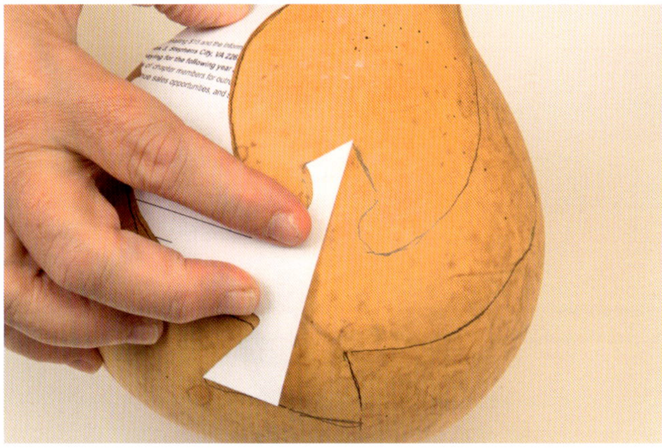

Draw the design on a gourd.

Cut out with a mini jigsaw or a handsaw.

Paint if you desire. At the very least, smooth the edges with a light sanding. Balance!

This is a banana gourd boat with a wire gourd man in it. When placing the balancing point of a skyhook on a shelf, the other side of the coat hanger is curved under the shelf as counterbalance.

BALANCE—BOAT SKYHOOK

Skyhooks are another way of using weight and gravity. They are centuries-old balancing toys made to sit on one point by using a curved counterbalance. In the 1800s skyhooks were commercially made with a sailor in a boat or a rider on a horse and sat on a shelf. The beauty part of these balancing toys is the curved wires extending beneath as a counterweight, which can be adjusted as needed to get the balance to work (Provenzo and Provenzo 1979, pp. 117–19). It's just a matter of translating this concept into "gourdspeak" by building the body from gourds and attaching the mechanisms for the motion, converting a traditional toy into a gourd in motion! This is an excellent way for children to learn about balance, and a stress-free way for crafters to make a toy work that looks delicate and complex at the same time!

To make any skyhook, cut a coat hanger in two places. One end will be the balancing point.

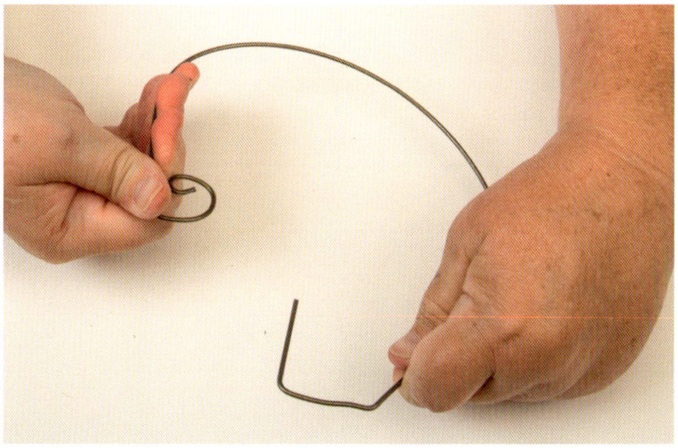

Use pliers to curl the other end for the counterbalance.

Cut open and gut a banana gourd to be a boat. Drill two holes—one at the backside and one on the bottom, toward the center of the boat.

Thread one end of the coat hanger through the hole at the backside and then through the center hole of the gourd to make a balancing point.

Use hot glue to secure a piece of scrap over the wire inside the boat, so the wire does not shift out of position.

Since balance is a process, keep in mind that when something is added to one part, there will need to be something done elsewhere for the balance work. When I added the wire man to the boat, the sail and gourd butterfly were necessary for equal the weight.

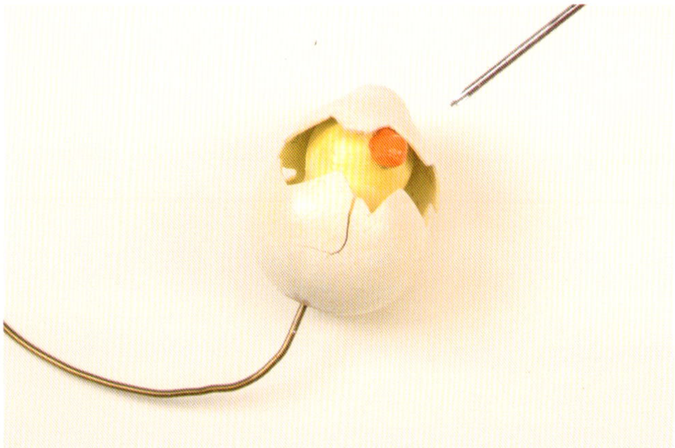

When I used this chicken UFO from the garage for a skyhook, the height and weight required adjustments for counterbalance. The addition of another UFO provided the weight necessary for balance. Don't be afraid to test and develop!

MOVING ENTERTAINMENTS

During the Renaissance, royalty and wealthy merchants who could afford to be entertained with novelties hired skilled artisans to make lifelike mechanical toys. These objects of mechanical science used increasingly complicated combinations of clockworks as patrons demanded more whimsy and realism (Gorman 1985). Automata, as they are called, have a long history, extending from 500 BCE to modern robotics (Race 2014). Also called kinetic sculpture, or mechanical toys, automata is the plural term for automaton (Onn and Alexander 1998)—an inanimate object brought to life with various parts and a cranking action. According to *The Oxford Companion to the Body* (Porter 2001), automata "in general inspire interest by their visual appeal, being intended to induce wonder and astonishment through the magic of their movement." I believe this to be true. Moving objects always catch my eye, and as I have worked through gourd possibilities, learning the properties and limitations of gourd wall structure, I have gravitated toward the magic of movement. These beginning steps for reinventing a gourd project are too simplistic for a person already involved with physics or engineering, but for people like me who use simple tools and gourd scraps, it is a fun way to make a little entertainment!

Automata Structure

An automaton has two fundamental parts: the frame, which is everything that creates the action, and the object(s) being moved. In this book, there will be housings made of wood to resemble a standard boxlike structure, and housings made from flat-bottomed gourds, tall enough to house moving parts yet sturdy enough to give unyielding support for the object(s) being moved. Even with instruction, be prepared to make adjustments as needed for parts to move smoothly. Gourds are a natural product, and no two will ever be alike. The same goes for wooden dowels—no two will be identical. As Anders Lunde (2003) advises in his book *Action Whirligigs*, "Just take the time to think about how it could go wrong, study the action and make adjustments."

FRAMES—A COLLECTION OF PARTS

A frame is a collection of parts with descriptive names that seem to define their functions: housing, crank, shaft, stops, driving mechanisms (which in this case will be cams), followers, and chasers. The frame's housing is the structural support of the automaton, holding the moving parts and supporting the object being moved. The crank is the handle that rotates the shaft, which is the horizontal rotating arm extending from side to side across the housing. Stops are small parts keeping the shaft from shifting out of position.

Cams are the driving mechanisms (Onn and Alexander 1998, pp. 59 and 97) we will use for this book. They are located on the shaft and rotate as the shaft turns. Cams can be easily made of pieces of gourd, or miniature gourds, and offer the biggest variety of movements for the effort. Think of a cam as a memory card driving the automaton action as the follower above "follows" the shape of the cam. The followers, connected to the object to be moved (Onn and Alexander 1998, p. 58) and inserted through holes at the top of the housing, are attached to chasers, which rest on the cams. Chasers should be a bit wider than the cam to ensure adequate contact.

The biggest tip for producing a frame, whether using wood or a gourd, is to make sure the drill bit matches the dowel size used for the other parts. I use the same size for everything, so the materials are consistent and I never have to worry if the bit in the drill is the right size. Bottom line, all automata work in the same way: As the crank turns a shaft, anything attached to it moves. Horizontal movement is converted into vertical movement. When that movement is connected to the gourd object above the housing, you have a gourd in motion!

A wooden housing is constructed with two sides, a top, and a base. Although glue is probably all that is required to hold the wood pieces together for a lightweight gourd

This gourd frame shows the key pieces of automata. In this case the gourd is the housing. The horizontal shaft holds the cams, which are threaded onto it to signal how the objects above the housing will move. Stops are added to the shaft on the outside of the housing to keep the shaft from shifting side to side. The crank is the handle that rotates the shaft. The chaser is the piece sitting on the edge of the cam as the shaft rotates. The follower is the vertical piece attached to the chaser at one end and to an object above the housing at its other end. Movement is transferred from the shaft and cam, to the chaser, through the follower, to the object being moved.

automaton, wooden dowels or toothpicks inserted at the glued areas add extra structural support in case it is dropped. The sides dictate the vertical space available for the parts inside the housing. Make sure the cams you intend to put on the shaft will fit inside the housing when rotated. The hole in each side wall for the shaft running from side to side should be as close to parallel as possible for adequate support.

The top needs to be long enough, and wide enough, to give the gourd objects being moved above the housing enough space to move without extending over the edges. It should also be thick enough so the followers can move up and down through it without leaning sideways or wobbling. Even with a correctly sized hole, a follower will tilt if the top is too thin. If this happens, reinforce the area by gluing extra pieces of wood or gourd onto the top, where the hole will be before drilling. This gives the follower added surface area for vertical support.

Make the base a little bigger and thicker than the sides and top in order to anchor the whole structure. Even though miniature gourds are lightweight, a too-narrow or insubstantial housing, compared to the objects being moved, makes the whole automaton top-heavy and prone to tipping over. Generally, the bigger or taller the automaton, the more substantial the base of the housing needs to be.

However, having said all this, do not overanalyze the first couple of automata. There is plenty of time to refine skills for a more polished result. At first, get some movement happening and have fun. Let's put some housings together.

Select pieces of wood for the housing frame that are at least ¼" thick: a top, two sides, and a base that's wider than the top.

Layer the sides. Make a light pencil X on the top one that crosses from corner to corner.

Drill a ¼" hole through both pieces of wood.

Glue the top onto the sides so the edges align.

Drill a small hole vertically through the top into each side.

Dot the hole with wood glue and put a matchstick into each hole for extra support.

Trim off extra matchstick and lightly sand.

Do the same for the base.

Use a string or tape to pencil a line on the top that will be parallel to the shaft, so the followers are directly over the cams on the shaft.

Use a string or tape to pencil a line on the top that will be parallel to the shaft, so the followers are directly over the cams on the shaft.

Slide a ¼" dowel through the side holes for a shaft.

Put a stop to one side of the shaft—this can be a piece of scrap glued onto the end as a cap, or a small matchstick wedged into a hole drilled through the end of the shaft.

Slide the shaft partially out and thread on a birdhouse hole scrap or mini gourd intended for use as a cam before going through the other side. Make sure to add a stop to keep the dowel from shifting from side to side within the housing.

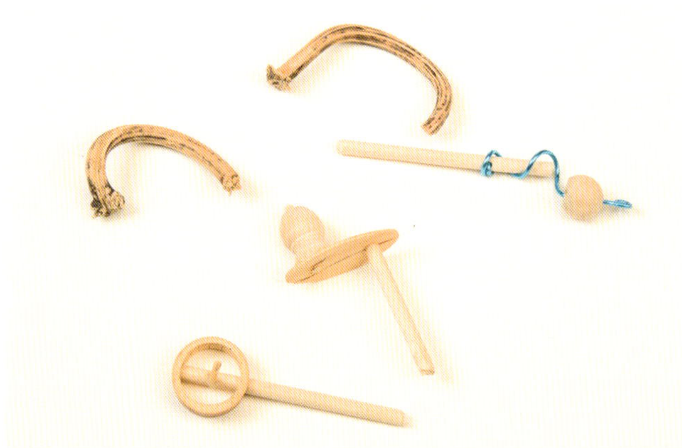

For a crank, there are many options. The goal is to make a handle you can rotate to turn the shaft.

First, trim off excess shaft dowel.

In this case, I drilled a hole to fit a toothpick for a handle.

A side note: craft stores and even the craft aisle at some big-box stores now sell wooden boxes—that wasn't the case when this book began. You could save a bit of time if you go that route.

A gourd housing is not as stable as a wood housing, mostly because of its light weight and flexible wall structure. However, the appearance is so unique that it is sometimes worth the extra effort to anchor it with a wood base for more stability. Start with a thick-walled canteen gourd, since the shape lends itself to a flat(ish) top and bottom, and the thick wall adds to the sturdiness of the final housing. Do NOT scrimp on breathing protection when it comes to gutting the gourd. Wear a two-canister respirator or at the very least a hospital mask, outside, in a well-ventilated area. Gourd dust is toxic and, as described earlier, is finer than wood dust and not desirable for nasal or lung passages.

Draw a line around two opposing sides of a canteen gourd, leaving enough gourd at the center, where the stem is, for a broad base. A bandsaw makes fast work of this process, but a mini craft saw, a coping saw, or a Dremel works fine. Use what you have on hand and be patient. If you find you like automata, upgrade and invest in different tools. Until then, go low-tech and simple or find a neighbor with tools who can help do this quickly.

Using a gourd to make a housing has some differences; the first is stability. Anchor the gutted gourd to a broad base such as a piece of wood by using wood glue or some other permanent adhesive.

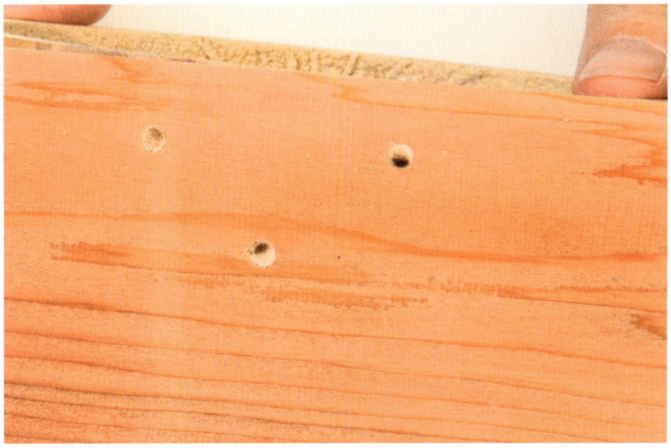

I generally drill two holes through the bottom of the gourd and wood for pieces of dowel to give extra support.

Dab the holes with glue before inserting the dowels.

Another difference will be the stops for the shaft. Make sure the shaft is, in fact, at the fattest point of the gourd belly, so the stops at either end of the crank are not catching against the gourd and stopping the action.

MAKING THE MOVEMENTS

Cams made from gourds can be shaped easily since the structure of a gourd wall is easy to cut and sand. I use the leftover scraps from birdhouse projects along with scraps from my stash of gourds and old projects. As a point of interest, gourd wall thicknesses can vary widely, even when grown in the same garden. Keep that in mind when selecting pieces of scrap to use, and when making choices to fit inside the housing.

When the entry hole is made with a drill bit for a hole saw, a round plug with a hole already drilled through the center is the leftover. A hole saw bit is a drill attachment holding another drill bit inside it to act as a guide for the hole. If the entering bit is the same size as the shaft and follower dowels, lots of time will be will saved. A hole saw bit can be purchased individually or in sets for holes of various sizes.

The movement possibilities of a cam depend on size and shape: the size determines the speed of the motion, and the shape determines the action of the automaton object. *Left to right*, these cam shapes produce basic motions: (1) spinning, (2) up and down, (3) rise and drop, and (4) jumping. Can you imagine which cam cannot be rotated backward?

If you imagined that number 3 and 4 cannot be rotated backward, you would be correct! If rotated backward, the chaser would snag on the sharp edge that makes the drop. That's something to consider when deciding how the crank is oriented to move the shaft.

When choosing scraps to make cams and chasers, be sure to select pieces to fit in the housing and still have enough body for adequate contact with other parts.

Birdhouse entry holes are generally cut with a hole cutter. These leftover pieces of gourd make the perfect scrap for cams because they already have the ¼" center hole!

These are the four cams I make from birdhouse hole scraps: round, egg or oval shaped, snail shaped, and sawtooth.

SPINNING

The spinning movement is, in my opinion, the most universal way to prompt gourd motion. In addition, centrifugal force will make anything dangling on the automaton move as the spinning action occurs. When designing your automaton, give some thought to the details, which can add a bit of whimsy as well as action. Earrings on a gourd doll, leaves on a tree, or loose legs add visual interest when the spinning makes those details fly out to the side.

Begin with a housing that is big enough to support the figure being moved. In this case, here is a small chicken with ribbon legs (beads as feet) and a similarly sized box from a craft store.

Make the holes for the shaft at the sides by making the cross and drilling the ¼" holes.

Check to make sure the birdhouse hole scrap will fit inside the box on the shaft.

Slide the wooden dowel shaft through one side hole and thread a cam onto it before going through the other side hole.

Find the centerline over the shaft and drill a follower hole.

Glue stops into place on the shaft at both sides of the housing, so it does not shift side to side within the box.

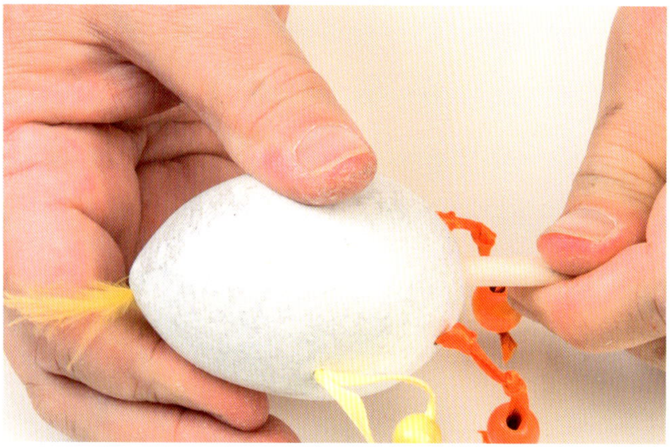

Drill a ¼" hole at the bottom of the chick and insert a ¼" dowel the full length of the chick.

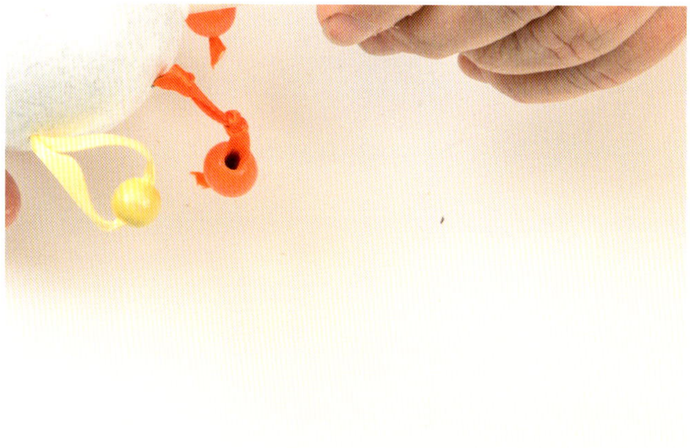

Back it out a little and apply glue before reinserting.

Tap the cam on the shaft into position—it should be slightly to one side of the follower hole.

Put the follower (the dowel with the chick) into the top hole to mark where the dowel needs to be trimmed. The chick should be at least ½"–1" above the housing and the end of the follower, level with the top of the cam.

Sometimes, if the housing is too thin, additional support will need to be added so the follower doesn't lean. In this case, I added another scrap on top of the housing for more vertical support.

Put a birdhouse hole scrap onto the end of the follower as the chaser, so the rough side is in contact with the rough edge of the cam. Do a test of the motion by turning the shaft. If a complete revolution does not work, adjust—usually by tapping the cam along the shaft or making the contact between the cam and chaser rougher for more friction.

When you are satisfied, back the follower out of the chase a little to put glue into the hole before reinserting it. Do the same with the cam on the shaft.

While that dries, add a crank. In this case, I made a wire handle.

UP AND DOWN

A simple up-and-down action is generated with an off-center hole. The scrap itself can be circular or oval (an egg cam), with an off-center shaft hole that provides the high/low variation as the shaft rotates. Using a whole miniature gourd adds an interesting cam variation when the hole is drilled diagonally across the gourd, so the shaft is NOT centered. When making the frame for this action, make sure the interior of the housing has enough vertical space to accommodate the fattest side of the cam, so there is space in the housing when rotated.

Begin with the kind of box we used before and one of the chicks we made earlier in the book—the one with the wire legs.

Shape the round cam into an egg shape, and sand the edge smooth.

Check the cam against a side hole to make sure it will fit inside the housing as it rotates. Since it is not round, make sure the fattest side will fit all around with a chaser on top of it.

Thread the cam onto the shaft as it passes through the housing from one side to the other.

Drill a hole into the bottom of the chick, and glue in a dowel so it extends the full length as done in the spinning project.

Add extra support to the top hole before inserting the follower.

This time, when positioning the cam, place it directly under the follower hole so the follower and chaser sit directly on top.

Mark the follower so it can be trimmed before adding the chaser.

Put the chaser onto the end of the follower, so the smooth side is against the cam. Make sure it all fits and moves when the fattest part of the cam is rotated up and down. Glue everything into position.

Add a crank and go up and down!

A similar action can be done with a miniature bottleneck gourd. Start with the same box, but instead of a cam made from a birdhouse entry hole scrap, drill a diagonal hole through a miniature bottleneck gourd. Thread the gourd onto the shaft.

RISE AND DROP

The rise-and-drop action is a movement made by a rise followed by an abrupt drop. A cam with an off-center hole becomes a snail cam when a right angle is cut to make a ledge. In fact, when looking at a snail cam it is obvious why it is so named. The right-angle cut becomes the starting point for a smooth curve that spirals toward the original edge. The curve eventually leads back to the ledge, which the chaser falls over abruptly, making a sudden drop. The deeper the cut is into the circle, the more pronounced the drop will be.

Make a housing and then a snail cam, with a deep cut on the edge of one of the birdhouse hole scraps.

Make a wire man, but only the head and arms. We're going to make a person who peeks out of something and then quickly hides again.

Drill a ¼" hole in the bottom of the gutted gourd—I'm using a bowl painted to look like a flower from an unfinished project in garage.

Align the flower's hole over the hole at the top of the housing, and glue it onto the housing.

Drill a small hole at the end a dowel to be used for the follower.

Attach the wire man to a follower by using a piece of wire wrapped through the man's shoulders and through the follower.

Thread the snail cam onto the shaft as it passes through the housing, so that the snail curve bends forward.

Remember to add stops so the shaft doesn't shift.

Position the cam directly under the holes in the top and flower bowl.

Take time to trim the follower so the man, at the topmost point of the cam, is showing only his eyes—mark the spot so it can be trimmed.

Add the chaser to the end of the trimmed follower, so the smooth side is in contact with the cam. Test to make sure it works before gluing the cam and chaser in place.

For the crank, drill a small hole through the shaft that's big enough to take a wire. This crank is wired with a gourd stem and artificial flowers.

OTHER AUTOMATA MOVEMENTS

Frequent jumpy, choppy, or jiggly movements are made with variations not only of size but of the cam's shape. By now you can probably figure out why, right? The movements are the result of the cam's edge, which are cut or sanded so the chaser and follower transfer the line of action to the figure being moved. Consider what action the figure needs to make, and test the shape to accommodate the movement.

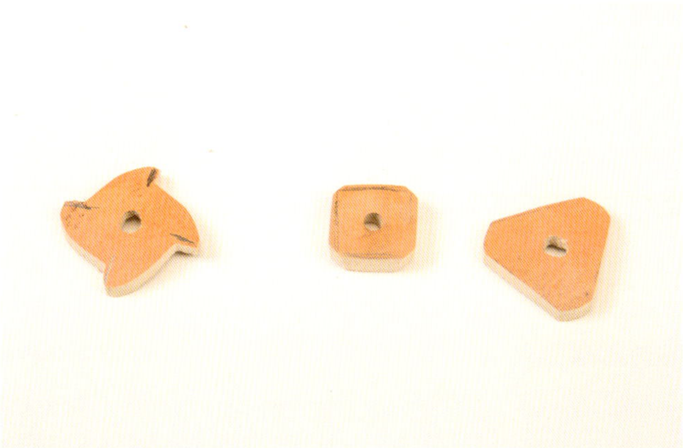

Cams can be sanded into shapes other than circles for other movements. The sawtooth provides a jumpy, jiggly motion, whereas a square is jumpy but not as frantic. A triangle-shaped cam jumps but is even more laid back than the square's motion because there are fewer corners.

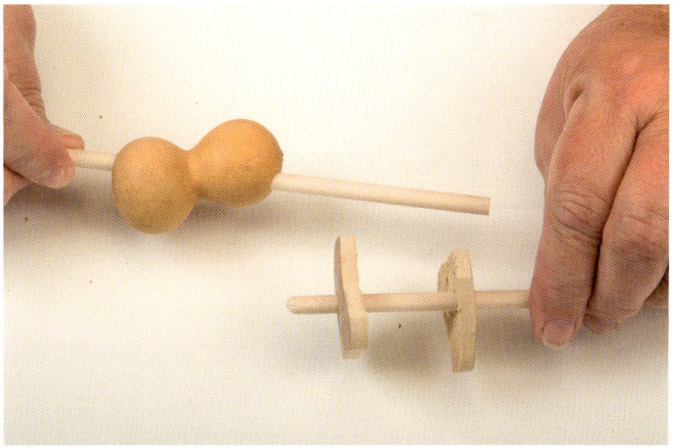

Here are two different cam setups that can produce the same movement. Both make an up-and-down motion for two chasers and followers. Again, use what you have on hand!

THE LAST WORD

Some words of wisdom for the beginner, and even for gourd enthusiasts who have a long history of working with gourds: be prepared to make adjustments as needed. Whether you are making old-fashioned toys or more-complicated automata, gourds are a natural product, and very few will be similar enough to mass produce projects. The same caution applies to wooden dowels, which can warp or be affected by heat and humidity. The label on a wooden dowel may say ¼", but there will be differences. If you understand this at the start, you will not be disappointed when some toys or automatons do not run smoothly initially. Metal gears that have been machined are going to be consistent and reliable. Natural products . . . not so much. Be flexible and willing to experiment if you hit a rough patch. Even after all my years of gourd work, I still test and redo to make a project work. People in the gourd patch I belong to have sat in my garage on work session nights, watching me go through trials and errors. Eventually there is success—you will have the joy of successes too!

Let me share some adjustments I have made as I worked through missteps.

In this project, the wire man peeking out of the flower did not rise enough to give a believable "peek" because the cam was too small. A larger circle provided a better lift for the follower.

The crank is a repurposed piece of gourd stem. However, it was too long and would not make a complete revolution, so it was cut to fit.

This was a lesson learned: I wanted the balancing bird to have wings that flapped upward, so I snapped them off and reglued them. However, that changed the center of gravity, so it would not balance. The wings were reattached because it turns out they must curve down.

In the triple-chicken automaton (*see* opposite page), one gourd cam was mismeasured and would not complete a revolution. The underneath area of the housing top where the cam rubbed had to be sanded to make a hollowed space, so the gourd cam would turn freely.

In the fish automaton (*see* cover), the shaft was not at the widest part of the gourd, so the crank snagged as it tried to turn the shaft. Gourd scraps were added as spacers, and then it all worked because the crank had enough room to rotate.

Also, for the same automaton, the followers did not have enough vertical stability and leaned forward and back. Supports were made from scraps, which acted as guides to keep the followers upright.

It is my dearest wish that this information inspires you to put motion into your gourd art. There's a bit of irony that gourds begin their lives moving along the ground and up trellises as they grow. The gourd plant is alive and green and full of movement. They come back to life when talented artisans create fantastic specimens of visual and tactile beauty. They can be especially delightful when they come back to life with physical movement. The mechanical systems presented in this book are basic and are intended to boost your personal path to exploring gourds. Keep learning, keep loving, and keep living the gourd life—have fun!

REFERENCES

Ballman, B. "Amid Days of High-Tech Playthings, Simplest Toys Still Racking Up Sales." *Capital District Business Review* 19, no. 9 (June 15, 1992). http://link.galegroup.com/apps/doc/A124514811TOF?u=va0072_remote&sid=ITOF&xid=6ef196c7.

Bledsoe, Helen Wieman. "Children in Colonial America Played with Homemade Toys." *Grit* 120, no. 1 (August 4, 2002): 6. http://link.galegroup.com/apps/doc/A90040645/ITOF?u=va0072_remote&-sid=ITOF&xid=a7711c46.

Bower, Bruce. "Ancient Kids' Toys Have Been Hiding in the Archaeological Record." *ScienceNews* 193, no. 3 (February 6, 2018a): 25. www.sciencenews.org/article/ancient-toys-kids-archaeological-record.

Bower, Bruce. "When It's Playtime, Many Kids Prefer Reality over Fantasy." *ScienceNews* 193, no. 3 (February 6, 2018b): 22. www.sciencenews.org/article/kids-play-fantasy-reality.

Gorman, Benjamin A. "Toys Are Us." Curriculum Unit 85.06.04. New Haven, CT: Yale Teachers Institute, June 4, 1985. http://teachersinstitute.yale.edu/curriculumunits/1985/6/85.06.04.x.html.

Lasky, Julie. "Designing Distraction: Executive Toys." *New York Times*, February 4, 2015. www.nytimes.com/2015/02/05/garden/designing-distraction-executive-toys.html.

Lee, Buddy. "Jump Rope by Any Other Name, Jumping Ropes, Rope Jumping, Skipping Rope, or Rope Skipping, It Is Still a Jump Rope." Jump Rope Institute. Retrieved May 8, 2018, www.jumpropeinstitute.com/History.htm, and confirmed via email May 25, 2018.

Lienhard, John H. "No. 1469: The Hourglass." Engines of Our Ingenuity. 1988. www.uh.edu/engines/epi1469.htm.

Lunde, Anders S. *Action Whirligigs: 25 Easy-to-Do Projects*. New York: Dover, 2003.

Mayotte, Rick. "Build a Folk Toy Acrobat." Video file, posted October 29, 2016. www.youtube.com/watch?v=V5803sJk4SQ.

McMahon, Felicia. "Toy." In *Encyclopaedia Britannica*. London: Encyclopaedia Britannica, May 15, 2014. www.britannica.com/technology/toy.

Medder, Ben. "Movement." Retrieved April 10, 2018, www.benmedder.com/movement/.

Mills, Alan A., S. Day, and S. Parkes. "Mechanics of the Sandglass." *European Journal of Physics* 17, no. 3 (1996): 95. https://doi.org/10.1088/0143-0807/17/3/001.

Onn, Aidan Lawrence, and Gary Alexander. *Cabaret Mechanical Movement: Understanding Movement and Making Automata*. London: Cabaret Mechanical Theatre, 1998.

Porter, Roy. "Automata." In *The Oxford Companion to the Body*. Edited by Colin Blakemore and Sheila Jennett. New York: Oxford University Press, 2001. Accessed via Encyclopedia.com: www.encyclopedia.com/medicine/encyclopedias-Almanacs-transcripts-and-maps/automata.

Provenzo, Eugene F., Jr., and Asterie Baker Provenzo. *Easy-to-Make Old-Fashioned Toys*. New York: Dover, 1979.

Race, Robert. "Introduction." In *Making Simple Automata*. Ramsbury, UK: Crowood, 2014.

Simmons, M. (2011, September 7). Craftsman out-spins them all. *Knoxville News Sentinel*. Retrieved from http://archive.knoxnews.com/news/local/craftsman

Tabler, Dave. "For Christmas—the Whimmydiddle or the Flipperdinger?" Appalachian History: Stories, Quotes and Anecdotes, November 30, 2015. www.appalachianhistory.net/2015/11/For-christmas-whimmydiddle-or.html.

Taylor, Jacques H. N. "Why Your Brain Is Made for Movement." *Life* (blog), October 1, 2011. www.huffingtonpost.com/jacques-henri-taylor/Mindful-movement_b_892955.html.

Wheeler, H. "Indigenous Spinning Top from Cape York, Pre-1900." Australian Museum, October 2, 2012. https://australianmuseum.net.au/learn/cultures/atsi-collection/cultural-objects/indigenous-spinning-top-from-cape-york-pre-1900/.